PRAISE FOR
BRAVE ENOUGH TO BE BROKEN

"Toni is a life-giving friend and leader. I'm sure you will leave time with her convicted and encouraged. She's somehow a blaze of fire and a big hug at the same time!"

—JENNIE ALLEN, *New York Times* BESTSELLING AUTHOR,
GET OUT OF YOUR HEAD AND *FIND YOUR PEOPLE*

"When healing past traumas and praying for hope to come, it can be easy to get discouraged. In *Brave Enough to Be Broken*, Toni gives a road map that guides you to healing and hope while her spunky and raw approach to writing helps you not feel alone along the way!"

—REBEKAH LYONS, BESTSELLING AUTHOR, *RHYTHMS OF RENEWAL*

"We are all broken in so many ways but, as Toni helps us understand, we can't begin to heal until we bring our pain into the light. In this honest, hope-filled book, Toni shares the truth that in God's hands what we thought would break us will be used to make everything new."

—SHEILA WALSH, AUTHOR, *HOLDING ON WHEN YOU WANT TO LET GO*

"It takes great effort to weave the threads of deep, transformational truth with those of our vulnerable, wounded life—and then present the fabric to the world as a tapestry of beauty. In Toni Collier, we have such a weaver. And, with *Brave Enough to Be Broken*, we have received, in thoughtful and immediately applicable ways, what we need, because we have received Toni herself, someone who knows what it means to do the hard work—perhaps the hardest work we have to do—of allowing God to love us. To heal, convict, and transform us in the ways only God can. For you who are broken, for you who longs to be brave, for you who hungers and thirsts to become more than you can imagine—read this book and live the courageous life that God has intended for you from before the creation of the world."

—CURT THOMPSON, MD; AUTHOR, *THE SOUL
OF DESIRE* AND *THE SOUL OF SHAME*

"I love Toni. I have come to know her as a radiant example of both the humility and beauty that is woven into every true redemption story. Pain has a purpose for those courageous enough to dig deep and find it. In a time when far too many people are struggling to maintain false images and idols that say they have it all together, Toni invites us to fall into the arms of Jesus and be Brave Enough to Be Broken. This message is so desperately needed because on the other side of true brokenness there is hope and healing."

—LISA BEVERE, *NEW YORK TIMES* BESTSELLING
AUTHOR OF *WITHOUT RIVAL*

"In *Brave Enough to Be Broken* Toni Collier invites us to face the broken pieces of our stories and discover how God can redeem every corner of our lives. Instead of sharing empty platitudes and unrealistic expectations, Toni vulnerably shares the story of her personal rock bottom and how God met her there. Then drawing on personal testimony, biblical insights and wise counsel, she leads us forward with practical tools that build a pathway into the future that God offers each one of us. If you're looking to rebuild your life choose (to be) *Brave Enough to Be Broken*. Toni will be a wise and kind guide for your journey."

—JO SAXTON, AUTHOR, *READY TO RISE*; FOUNDER,
EZER COLLECTIVE; LEADERSHIP COACH

"*Brave Enough to be Broken* isn't just a catchy title, it's the life I have seen my friend Toni lead. Her bravery is visible over her whole life, and she has graciously shared that here in this book with all of us. Toni leads us all so well with her words—going first with her own story and then pointing us all toward the path of healing. I pray as you devour each word, you will witness God doing a mighty work in your own life."

—JAMIE IVEY, BESTSELLING AUTHOR AND HOST OF
THE HAPPY HOUR WITH JAMIE IVEY PODCAST

BRAVE
ENOUGH
TO BE
BROKEN

BRAVE ENOUGH TO BE BROKEN

HOW TO EMBRACE YOUR PAIN AND DISCOVER HOPE AND HEALING

TONI COLLIER

NELSON BOOKS

An Imprint of Thomas Nelson

Published in Nashville, Tennessee, by Nelson Books, an imprint of Thomas Nelson. Nelson Books and Thomas Nelson are registered trademarks of HarperCollins Christian Publishing, Inc.

Published in association with The Bindery Agency, www.TheBinderyAgency.com

Thomas Nelson titles may be purchased in bulk for educational, business, fundraising, or sales promotional use. For information, please email SpecialMarkets@ThomasNelson.com.

To my daughter, Dylan—the girl who gave me a reason to fight for healing beyond my own desire for peace. This book is proof that while the hardest thing I've ever done was healing my own childhood wounds while raising you, I didn't give up. My prayer is that when you read these words, you will have learned how to embrace pain and find healing and hope in your own life by how I lived my life in front of you.

CONTENTS

CONTENTS

AN INVITATION TO BECOME BRAVE

The greatest gift I've ever given myself was the bravery to press into pain and the freedom to heal from it. And it's exactly what I want for you.

I'm proud of you for picking up a book with a title like this one. It almost feels like an oxymoron, doesn't it? Like brave and broken shouldn't be in the same sentence. But you picked this up for a reason. Maybe you're in a season when you feel absolutely broken. You've tried to mend that relationship, not let the anxiety cripple you, stay away from the abuse and toxicity, and maybe you've really searched for a better way to be happy. Maybe you've begun to realize that your negative responses aren't just happening because you didn't like a certain situation, but because one moment in it triggered a past moment in your childhood that damaged you deeply. So you picked up this book. Maybe because for the first time you are ready to face the pain that has caused so much brokenness in your life, and heal from it. (Or maybe you just thought it had a cute cover.)

I am sorry that you've endured so much pain. In this world, we will experience heartbreak. It's inevitable. That means most of us are walking around wounded, feeling the pain of being deeply broken human beings. I am a deeply broken human being. Your pastor is a deeply broken human being. Your favorite person in the world is a deeply broken human being. Your hero is a deeply broken human being. Your husband, child, boss, founder, CEO, friend, and confidant are all deeply broken human beings. But each of us is still so worthy of love and belonging.

I've seen that pain can quickly turn into doubt. Doubting the goodness of humanity. Doubting that we deserve a gentle love.

Doubting that God's goodness is meant for us. Doubting that there's relief on the other side. And when doubt turns to disdain for the pain we suffer, we're tempted to numb our pain.

We don't want to feel pain fully. So we stay in toxic relationships by sweeping our emotions under the rug, or we self-sabotage so no one can get close and hurt us again. Or we use substances to numb ourselves—wine, drugs, essential oils, shopping, exercise, and more. Now, I'm not saying that all those things are bad; I'm simply emphasizing that we can use these things as crutches to numb the very emotions we need to feel in order to heal the very broken places we're hiding from the world—and ourselves.

I confess that I've numbed myself with all those things because I had unmet needs, anxiety, and deep pain.

As the queen Brené Brown says, "We *cannot* selectively numb emotion. If we numb the dark, we numb the light. If we take the edge off pain and discomfort, we are, by default, taking the edge off joy, love, belonging, and the other emotions that give meaning to our lives."[1] If we truly are to experience the greatest joy, we have to allow ourselves to fully experience our pain. We have to acknowledge the painful truths of our stories.

So I want to ask you, sister, what was it you needed? What hurt you? What kept you up at night? What gave you anxiety? What were you afraid of? Who hurt you? What pain cut so deeply that you didn't think you could be redeemed from it?

We all needed something that we didn't receive from the people who should have given it to us. Psychiatrist Curt Thompson says it best: "We are all born into this world looking for someone looking for us."[2] Someone and *some places* that would offer us security, comfort, safety—help to heal.

The world has made most of us believe that we're strong enough all by ourselves to overcome every hurdle we face. But, friend, that's simply not true. In fact, it's the very reason why I created an organization called Broken Crayons Still Color. I wanted to build something that not only provided community and closeness so women wouldn't feel so alone in their pain but also equipped those women with resources and strategies to overcome brokenness and find real healing and hope. When women find Broken Crayons, they are met in their darkest valleys of despair, but they're not *left* there. We now help women process brokenness and get to hope through online community, courses, resources, and events both live and virtual. We serve all women who are feeling broken and disqualified and are looking for hope. Our team believes that the world has lied to us: it has planted a narrative deep in our feminine hearts that perfection is the gatekeeper to action, success, and influence. In God's kingdom that's just not true.

In her book *Find Your People*, Jennie Allen says, "I believe that God is asking you and me to let people into our daily lives, into our deepest struggles, into our sin, into our routines, into our work, and into our dreams."[3] Why? Because when we let people into every aspect of our lives, we close the gaps of secrecy where shame typically sets in. We allow people to see the fulness of our weaknesses and choose to love us through it. Jennie and I agree: that's where the magic happens. And it's the journey I'm inviting you to embrace in these pages.

What if you were told that love and healing are available to you, despite your mistakes and despite your darkness? Galatians 6:2 says that we should "Carry each other's burdens, and in this way, you will fulfill the law of Christ." God commands us to be there, hand-in-hand, side-by-side, pressing into the pain for and with each other. Wherever you find yourself on this journey toward love, hope, and healing, I want to join you.

Part of this process is identifying the lie that has kept us stuck for so long. And if there was a scheme of the Enemy that could take us all out, it would be the lie that we have to be perfect when, in fact, the opposite is true: success is contingent not upon perfection but upon our surrender.

So welcome. In these pages I will get gut-level honest about where I have been personally, how I was radically changed, and how you and I can find joy and become an important part of God's plan, even with all our brokenness. More importantly, you will have the opportunity to journey through your own healing by God's grace. When I wrote this book, the one thing I wanted to do was to make sure that it was something you could come back to throughout your healing journey. I'd love for you to consider this your playbook. Your roadmap. When you are in pain or your heart and spirit feel sick, you can come back to this, unfold the pages that you have curled at the corners, search for your favorite highlighted and underlined words, and let me coach you through whatever you're going through.

The book is broken into three parts. In part one, I offer up some of the most painful parts of my story for one reason: *so you know you're not alone.* And in part two you'll find a unique healing roadmap created with you in mind. It's a step-by-step guide to steer you into the healing God wants for you with practical steps for your journey. Last, in part three we'll walk through moving forward in hope. Life can look very different when you've done deep, intentional work on your healing, so I wanted to make sure you are equipped to keep going after you read the last words of this book.

Welcome to the journey of bravely rewriting your narrative. I am confident that God can take all our messes—mine and yours—and still use them. I've seen it in the thousands of women in our organization, and I can't wait to see it in you.

Welcome to a journey of choosing to be brave enough to be broken.

Be brave, gal. Redemption will look so good on you.

Toni

PART 1

EMBRACING BROKENNESS LEADS TO HOPE

P art 1 of this book was the hardest to write. It's my story. The real hard parts of it. But I figured if I was going to lead you to dive into a life of bravery by embracing pain and finding hope and healing, I needed to go first. This part of the book, I believe, will help you realize that you're not in this alone; there are other women, including myself, who have chosen this path. If God was with me through it all, He'll be with you too.

CHAPTER 1

IN THE VALLEYS

WHEN THE PAIN JUST DOESN'T GO AWAY

Please, God, why does my life have to be so hard? Please, just take the pain away. I don't want to feel this anymore."

The weight of twenty-five years came crashing down as the trauma, the abuse, the feelings of being unprotected, betrayed, and used crushed me.

I was at the bottom of the stairs in the home I shared with my daughter, curled up with my knees suffocating my chest and my fingers clenching the opposite sides of my arms. And I was rocking back and forth. With every tilt forward, tears fell down my face, over my cheeks, onto my neck. Back and forth . . . tears. Back and forth . . . more tears.

It was as if I were physically trying to hold every part of my life together. Kind of like scooping up a big pile of laundry, and the socks and undies keep slipping out of the bottom. I thought, *If I could just squeeze tightly enough, things wouldn't unravel anymore. The bottom would stay in.*

I'd just gotten off a FaceTime call with my parents to discuss when my daughter, Dylan, would leave "grandparents' camp" in Texas to come back home to me in Georgia. The truth is, it had been hard to call my parents for help. I still felt the sting of wanting to make my dad proud. And I hadn't even begun to process the childhood wounds that dug deep into my performer's heart from taking care of my mom after she'd suffered a massive stroke when I was eight. Picking up the phone three months earlier to tell my parents that I couldn't bear the weight of abuse and poverty anymore was one of the most embarrassing moments of my life. Regardless, they took care of Dylan for me during my divorce, job loss, and transition from a toxic church environment that summer. They wanted to enjoy their only long-distance grandchild, but they also knew I needed to spend time alone, getting my life back together.

When my mom visited me before I sent Dylan with them for the summer, I saw her trying not to get caught looking at my shaking hands, a symptom of the crippling anxiety and post-trauma distress I'd developed. I could see in my mom's face that she was heartbroken for me, but our relationship and bond was barely surviving because of the distance I'd put between us. She knew the pain I was walking through. She'd gone through a physically abusive marriage before my dad and smelled the aroma of "I've had enough" (of my own toxic marriage), all over me. Her brief visit was hard. I knew she'd overheard me losing my temper with Dylan as I tried to parent while traumatized. I'd felt so ashamed. I still felt like a complete failure. I assumed that there would now never be a moment when my parents would be proud of me.

And as I lay crumpled at the foot of the stairs, I could almost see the bottom of my own life metaphorically falling out. I was so exhausted, so weak from the abuse, manipulation, and loneliness, all my body could do was collapse. It was playing out like a movie in my mind. I could see eight-year-old Toni in the front seat of the Chevy Suburban. I was peeking through tears into the rearview mirror, watching my brother hold my mom in the back seat as she was having her first stroke.

It was a Saturday, game day, and I had my gold-and-black JetStar cheerleading uniform on. Little Toni thought, *What's life going to be like without a mom? Who's going to do my hair?* Now, as a single mother of a one-year-old girl, I remembered being with my mom at doctor's appointment after doctor's appointment and hospital visit after hospital visit. I could see myself at the breakfast bar, opening the medicine organizer, and sliding my mom's Monday pills in. I saw young Toni trying to numb her pain with alcohol and marijuana at age thirteen and fourteen. And as I looked at my teen years I saw that Toni seeking validation from men through sex because she didn't feel accepted by her dad.

I remembered the toxic marriage that young-adult Toni had endured—the yelling back and forth and the door I watched being ripped off the hinges and the holes punched in the walls by someone I believed I was safe with. I saw poverty and the WIC and food stamps. The financial assistance from the church she worked at. I heard more yelling, and I saw the stack of plates shattered after being clobbered with a fist.

I witnessed the church that was supposed to be a refuge turn toxic because of the leader. I saw the spiritual manipulation and abuse of that leader who was more broken than his pride and prosperity allowed him to admit.

I saw the daughter of that Toni-in-crisis who was born into pain. Breastfed out of necessity because formula costs money.

Then I saw myself sitting at IHOP again with a stack of ninety-seven divorce papers, filling in every line because that Toni couldn't afford a lawyer. But she knew she needed a life of peace and stability for her daughter and for herself.

And in that moment, at the bottom of the stairs, the bottom had fallen out. I'd fallen apart, crushed by life's blows.

It just didn't make sense to me. I didn't understand why my life had to be so hard. Why my story had so many scars to heal. Wasn't there a God who cared for me? I'd gone to church, been saved at twenty-one, and had served the church tirelessly. I'd been ordained, spoken to students across Georgia, had eight different jobs at a church, and sacrificed by only getting paid for one. I *knew* God.

But right there at the bottom of the stairs, I was questioning *everything*. I was a good person, but for some reason I kept ending up in situations of trauma and abuse with people I trusted and loved. It felt like no matter what I did, no matter how much I tried, the bottom still fell out. For the first time in my life I realized that I'd been drowning for years but didn't know it. And when I came up for air so I could look at what had been drowning me, I ran out of oxygen.

Maybe this is you *now*. Maybe you're suffering today, stinging from the wounds of the past.

Or maybe that *was* you, but you had to keep going so you numbed it all, stuffed everything back in the pile, and kept carrying it. Maybe you've endured a divorce. Or disordered eating. Or church hurt.

Maybe you're in a season, now, of processing your brokenness. You're asking, "Why does it have to be so hard? I'm tired and I don't know how to get out of this. I don't know where to start; it's all so overwhelming. Maybe I deserve this; maybe it's because of my mistakes. Has God forgotten me? Will this always be my life?"

If you're reading this as a mom, you may be scared for your children. Scared that all your brokenness will leak onto them and one day the bottom will fall out for them.

Maybe reading this book is your last attempt at staying on this earth. Maybe you don't want to take another breath. But you picked up this book because there was something in you that wanted to continue to fight. I know the pain of hopelessness but still holding on to a tiny sliver of hope that maybe this could be the moment my life will be redeemed.

Or you might be thinking that you shouldn't keep reading because your story hasn't been hard in these same ways. Sis, beware of the pain comparison trap! Comparing your pain to the pain of others is always a losing game. Whatever you hold in your story is worthy of redemption.

Wherever you are, I see you.

After a while on the floor, my fingers loosened and my knees uncurled. Having finally allowed my emotions to be expressed, I felt a bit of release. After looking over my life and all the pain, I felt . . . *better*. (Even though I know that sounds unlikely.) I think as I was witnessing the bottom fall out, I chose to do the one thing I hadn't yet done: *surrender*.

For the first time I realized that I couldn't get through it alone. I couldn't carry the weight of all the trauma, abuse, and shame and still have hope. I had been holding all this by myself because I didn't think I was worthy to have anyone share the burdens I'd been carrying. And in that moment, when I couldn't carry it myself, I turned to God, and I pleaded. "Please, please take the pain away. Please, God, why does my life have to be so hard? Please take the pain away."

And for a moment I think He did take the pain away. For a moment I imagined God being on the sidelines of my life saying, "Put Me in the game, Toni. For twenty-five years I've been wanting to carry this for you. Put Me in; I've got strength for your weakness. I've got power for your brokenness. Put Me in the game."

That was also the day that I decided to find a counselor. I had felt for a while that I should try therapy, but I was scared. In my family, and in my culture, counseling was frowned upon as only for the "crazies" with "psychotic issues." But as I surrendered all my mess at the feet of Jesus, I knew God was leading me to get some help.

Also on that day I started to examine my community. As cliché as it sounds, you really do become who you're around. As I looked at my life, I realized I was in relationship with people who weren't healthy for me to be around; none of them were pointing me to healing and wholeness.

Healing and wholeness are what God wants for us. It's what He longs for. He wants us to go to Him when we're hurting and allow Him to step in with holy comfort. He wants nothing more than to show us the way from brokenness to hope. Not because He needs us to or it makes Him feel better about Himself, but because He genuinely wants to help us. I believe God wants healthy, healed, whole, and holy people walking around this earth.

The apostle Paul addressed this in 2 Corinthians. For a bit of context, the apostle Paul started off as a "religious bully" named Saul. He condemned people for believing in Jesus and sent them to prison, breaking up families because of their beliefs. He caused a lot of people a lot of pain. And I bet if we were to have a chat with Paul when he realized what he'd done, he would probably have felt a lot like us: way too broken to be comforted and accepted by God. Way too "messed up." But he had an encounter with God where the Lord spoke to him and said, "Bro, why are you tripping?" Okay, he probably didn't say it like that, but that was the gist of it. "Saul, why are you persecuting my people? I have something greater for you. I want to use you" (Acts 9:3–5, paraphrased).

And after God stopped Saul on this dirt road to have this conversation, Saul went to the place God had instructed him to go. But in that encounter God had allowed him to be blinded, to become helpless. Imagine one day walking around making calls and leading the charge, living your best life, and suddenly you can no longer see. It's crippling and scary, and you'd probably feel completely helpless.

But right there in the middle of Saul's helplessness—and I'm assuming curiosity about what was next—God spoke to him. Because in spite of Paul's story, God wanted to be a part of writing the rest of it with him (Acts 9:6–19).

About twenty years later, Paul was writing his second letter to the church in Corinth after a long journey of church planting and evangelism. The Corinthians had come to know Jesus but they'd become "fans" rather than "followers of God." They were fans of Jesus, clapping in the stands but unwilling to get in the game and do the hard work of what it meant to follow Him. The believers in Corinth were persecuting other Christians and being boastful and prideful. They weren't all the way in.

Paul wrote a letter to them reminding them of where their strength came from. In 2 Corinthians 11, Paul talked about boasting in a sarcastic way. He talked about how wise he was and how much he'd done. How he'd worked and been in prison and gotten beaten and been exposed to death again and again. He went on about how he'd labored and gone without sleep, been hungry and thirsty. He talked about how he should be the one boasting here. But instead, he boasted about something else: *his weakness*. In chapter 12, Paul boasted about the thorn in his flesh from Satan that tormented him and how he pleaded with God to take it away from him.

We know what it's like to plead too, Paul.

"Please take it away from me."

God responded to Paul and said, "My grace is sufficient for you, for my power is made perfect in weakness" (2 Corinthians 12:9). Paul wrote in response, "Therefore I will boast all the more gladly about my weaknesses, so that Christ's power may rest on me. That is why, for Christ's sake, I delight in weaknesses, in insults, in hardships, in persecutions, in difficulties. For when I am weak, then I am strong" (vv. 9–10).

Paul knew what I know today and what I pray you know or will learn as you journey through this book: everything that you've been through, everything that's tried to take you out, everything that you are holding, gives you access to hope. You've likely heard this saying before: "Our test is our testimony, and our messes are our miracles."

A lot of us have experienced this firsthand. We've known moments of complete desperation. Whether it was because we didn't study for a test that was coming up or we were longing for a family member to receive healing, we pleaded with Jesus. And that's our most vulnerable, sacred place. We may find ourselves curled up in balls when we can't handle our lives anymore. It's when we've run out of hope and grit and we feel scared and alone. And most of us get there only when we can no longer hold the bottom in place. When we get to places of complete desperation and ill health.

And the truth is, many of us become the toxic people we need saving from. When we ignore our pain we inadvertently resist the healing we need. So where does all that pain funnel into? Bad behaviors—trauma leakage in how we respond to and interface with people. We can begin to live out of our brokenness instead of our healing and really hurt the people we love because of it. And sometimes it's only in those moments that we go to God and invite Him in. But what would it look like if we lived a life of *boasting* about our weaknesses as our normal strategy? What if those curled-up balls looked more like a chosen posture of kneeling in prayer? What if instead of trying to maintain the perfect picture, shoving the dirty parts out of frame because we're ashamed for someone to see them, we gave them to a Savior who sees us through and through? The truth is, the formula doesn't change. Whether we're on the defense in complete desperation or bravely living a life on the offense—inviting God off the sidelines onto the fields of our lives—that formula still works. Our weakness can be exchanged for His power. Our broken-ness for His strength.

I wonder if, today, you're like me at the foot of the stairs. Maybe you're so tired of everything falling apart that you're finally ready to live a life on the offense.

In the past, I would plead for God to take away the pain. Today I pray for God to be with me in the pain as He and I journey toward hope. Because I know God didn't promise me a life of perfection; He promised He would be with me in the imperfection. He was with me when I transitioned away from a toxic community into a community that could hold life with me and point me back to Him. And I will testify that He was with me when I met my future husband, Sam, who urged me to go to counseling, and He was with me every week for those two years I did. He was with me in my sixteen-week be-trayal trauma group. He was with me as I went through EMDR (eye movement desensitization and reprocessing trauma treatment). He was with me at spiritual encounters and retreats. And He's here with me now as I offer you the road map that I, and many others, have used to brave the broken places.

OUR WEAKNESS CAN BE EXCHANGED FOR HIS POWER. OUR BROKENNESS FOR HIS STRENGTH.

Keep going! And don't abandon your brokenness. Bring it with you as you read, because you don't have to show up already healed here. That would be fake anyway. Bring your trauma and your pain and your abuse, your doubts, your fears, your insecurity, and all of your mess. Because Jesus wants it—all of it. He's so ready for you to tag Him in. He's ready for you to trade your weakness for His power, your brokenness for His strength. I know it's true because He did it for me. And over the years He's done it for the women I've had the privilege to lead and steward.

I believe that Jesus is in the valleys with us, but even more than that He wants to give us every tool to claw our way out. He's smart. And because He is the Creator of all and is working through and in everything, not only is He spiritually present with us in every moment but He's also giving us the practical tools to live redemption out day by day. If you're ready to do the work, hope and healing can be yours.

CHAPTER 2

SOMETHING'S LEAKING

WHEN WE NAME IT, IT CAN BE HEALED

I love donuts.

Like, a whole bunch.

Specifically, Shipley Do-Nuts in Texas. There's something about the original glaze that rocks my world. But when I was introduced to the snacks in vending machines in middle school, my favorite donut quickly became the small six-pack of Hostess white powdered donuts. Back then, we didn't have the great healthy snacks in the vending machines like the kids do now. We had the real stuff: soda, candy, and my favorite—the white powdered donut. I couldn't wait to sit down for lunch with my friends on that hard lunch bench. I'd eat my pizza with the square pepperoni, whatever fruit they'd plopped onto our trays, and my prized possession, the donuts. My favorite memory was when they'd get stuck to the roof of my mouth and I had to take my finger and claw it out. Real attractive!

I remember one day I was sitting with my friends doing the regular routine at lunch, eating my donuts, when I had to use the bathroom. I got up, glared at all my friends, counted my donuts— one, two, three, four—and headed out.

As I skipped back to the table from the bathroom, I squinted at the plastic pack of white delicacies, "One . . . two . . . three." Someone had eaten one of my white powdered donuts. I lost it. I mean I really lost it.

I started yelling at my friends. "Who ate my donut? Who ate my donut?!"

My anger turned into yelling that turned into a wild scream that only rage and hurt could produce. Things escalated and I found myself standing on that lunch bench, yelling at my group of friends to 'fess up and tell me who ate my donut. And then I locked eyes with one of my best friends who hadn't said a word and whose mouth had been weirdly sealed shut.

I looked over at her and asked, "Nicole, did you eat my white powdered donut?"

She burst out laughing and white powder spewed all over the table.

I lost it. Again. I screamed at her and told her to take her finger and scrape my donut off the roof of her mouth.

Seconds later the vice principal, a slender African American woman who knew me well, tapped on my shoulder and asked me to come to her office. The table filled up with "Ooohs" as I stepped one foot after the other and walked through the cafeteria looking down at the tile floor until it turned into the carpet that welcomed me into the vice principal's office. As soon as we sat down, the unraveling of the white powdered donut saga began.

"Antoinee', you're a great student. What's going on?" she asked gently. (Antoinee' is my legal name.)

"Nothing," I replied. Giving the typical preteen answer that translates to *I'm lying and don't want to tell you.*

She was unfazed.

"You're captain of the cheerleading team, you're on student council, you're a part of the drama team's Thespian Society, and you work here in my office on your off period. I know you and you're a good student. Can you share with me why you were yelling and standing on the cafeteria table?"

"Nicole ate my white powdered donut!" I blurted out.

"And that's why you were yelling and crying? And standing on Harris County property? One white powdered donut?" she asked, knowing there was more.

"Well, it was *my* white powdered donut, and she didn't even ask and—"

She cut me off. "Antoinee', I would love for you to share what's really going on," she said as she placed her hand on my shoulder.

It seems like every time someone does the sentimental touch on the shoulder, the real stuff comes out, doesn't it? I burst into tears and sobbed. My head bowed down low; my shoulders were shaking. And even though I could've told her everything that was going on, I lied and told her I'd just gone through a bad breakup.

The truth was that my mom had been in and out of the hospital, and there I was, balancing her health and school and seeking validation from my dad.

After my mom's first stroke when I was in the third grade, sickness had plagued her body. One massive stroke was followed by three ministrokes, blood clots in her legs, her large intestine failing, carpal tunnel surgery in both hands, seizures, and so much more. I'd helped her get to doctors' appointments, held her hair and made sure she didn't swallow her tongue during bad seizures. I'd spent nights in the hospital feeding her and making sure the doctors did what they were supposed to. And I was scared. I was scared every night that I would wake up without a mom. That she would be taken from me.

So when Nicole took my white powdered donuts, it triggered me. Those were *my* white powdered donuts. And with the threat of the most important person being taken away from me being a daily fear, I was deeply attached to the things I could control. The things that I held close, big or small.

If you know what it feels like to be stuck in a cycle of trauma, to be "bossed around" by old pain, perhaps you're feeling like little Antoinee' right now. The way I coped was by trying to control what I could. What were the ways you struggled to survive? Maybe you retreated into a safe space. Maybe you turned your anger toward others. Maybe you bit your nails. Or cut yourself. Maybe today you're shopping and spending to soothe that pain. Whatever your coping mechanism of choice, believe me, I get it. In fact, I understand exactly why you'd want to keep your pain hidden—from others and maybe even from yourself. As a girl, you were smart about what you needed. And you figured out how to soothe yourself. But as you matured, those little girl–sized defenses didn't fit anymore. The ones you thought would help you might now be hindering you, keeping you from a healed and whole life.

But this book wasn't written to shame you about the decisions you've made to survive the pain you've been through. Rather, I want to encourage you to bring all your pain to light. We need to bring our pain into the light because it's in the light where healing and hope are found. The truth is that unhealed trauma will keep impacting us. We can't run from it. Our minds, hearts, and bodies weren't made for it, and so we are consciously and unconsciously clawing our way to relief and refuge. Our bodies want freedom and true hope. And when we don't find that, the very things we use to numb the pain become the choices that can harm us. At some point our bodies will give out. When we haven't learned healthy ways to heal from our pain, we end up medicating ourselves to an internal death.

WE NEED TO BRING OUR PAIN INTO THE LIGHT BECAUSE IT'S IN THE LIGHT WHERE HEALING AND HOPE ARE FOUND.

I remember the moment young Toni started to die inside. When she lost her awe and wonder for the world and stopped playing. When even her longtime friends who used to call her a "Teletubby" because she was so consistently joyful, saw her light start to dim. It was a distinct and dark turn that took me years to recognize. I was thirteen.

It was the last day of my freshman year in high school. My parents had gone to Louisiana to visit family and were still driving back home when I got out of school. I invited my secret boyfriend, who was way too old for me, over to our house. We'd been trying to have sex all year, but it wasn't working. The pain was too great.

I didn't want to be a virgin anymore because I thought if it happened, he would stay with me—that he would show me the affection that I sought desperately. I needed to feel a sense of accomplishment too, and I thought maybe he'd show me that he was proud of me. Then on the last day of school we were in my bedroom trying again as his best friend sat in our living room, and that day it worked. I remember being so happy, so pleased with myself. We kissed one last time before he left. Then I closed the door and locked it. I also closed the door on young Toni. Her childhood innocence, her awe and wonder, were now locked out.

My desire to be noticed and seen turned into twerking at parties so all the boys would dance with me and all the girls would be jealous. I turned to drugs and getting drunk until I couldn't remember the nights of partying. My rage leaked out as I punched walls and defied my parents. My longing to be beautiful and skinny turned into bulimia, so I could eat what I wanted without keeping it down long enough to absorb too many calories.

Still today, I sometimes get mad that no one saw how much I was hurting or offered to help. And then I get upset with myself about shaking off my tears and lying to the vice principal about where my pain was coming from. Maybe she would have helped me start a healing process the day of the white powdered donut saga and I wouldn't have sunk even further into a shame cycle, winding deeper and deeper down into a lifestyle of coping that I didn't think I could escape from.

I became the party girl, but really I was the broken girl trying to escape the realities of her life. I was on social media pretending that life was good so often that I inadvertently convinced my own heart of the same. My dangerous and damaging coping tactics numbed me. I had bought into what the Enemy often tries to plant in our hearts: *You're too broken to be fixed. You're too blemished to start over. You're already canceled.* The Enemy had his eye on me even before I accepted Jesus into my heart. He thought if he could plant these lies into my heart at an early age, I'd never feel worthy enough for refuge and redemption. Boy, was he wrong.

With maturity and hindsight, I can now look back over those school years and recognize how some of my behaviors were responses to the trauma I'd endured. At the time, I convinced myself that I was living my best life, but I can see that the pain I was unable or unwilling to face was driving my behavior. My trauma was still the boss of me.

Today, when I speak from the stage, I'm pretty comfortable naming some of these expressions of the hurt that was bubbling inside me. The donut freakout. The aggressive twerking and dancing at parties and clubs. Soothing my feelings with weed and a Taco Bell chalupa. I can see that because I was desperate for my father's approval, joining the middle school swim team and coming close to drowning in my first meet was yet another way I tried to cope. And the crowds laughed. But I think I can laugh now because I've sat in my counselor's office and cried about it. The difference? *I've healed from it now.* And I've healed from it because I've named it. If we're going to heal from it, we've got to name it. I was willing to get down in the trenches of my story and name the things that broke me so I could get to a place of wholeness. I fought through the shame of hiding these broken parts of my story and eventually mustered up the courage I needed to walk into conversations with safe community and counselors that could help me heal. I clawed my way to hope.

And I suspect that the reason you're reading this book is because you want that too. You want to be able to look back at the stories that have caused you the greatest pain and say, "It hurt like hell, but my wounds are now my scars of honor. I've healed from you."

IF WE'RE GOING TO HEAL FROM IT, WE'VE GOT TO NAME IT.

Maybe you haven't had the courage and support you've needed to name those things that have hurt you deeply. Maybe you're afraid to name your wounds because if you do you won't be able to hide them anymore. You might be afraid they will break you if they are exposed. You may have had some incredibly painful things happen in your story, which you have tried so hard to ignore that you can barely remember them. But, friend, I've got to let you in on this. If you want to move forward, if you want to live a life of healing and wholeness, you have to name your wounds. Your secrets have more control over you when they're hidden—I promise.

Maybe someone you trusted touched you in a way that little girls shouldn't be touched. Or maybe you lost the daily presence of the parent you loved—to divorce, abandonment, or death. Maybe you lived in a home where the person who should have been protecting and nurturing you was suffering from an addiction or mental illness. I encourage you to pause, this evening or this weekend, to take inventory of what you endured as a child. Notice the ways you were affected by someone's presence. Notice how you were shaped by someone's absence. Notice the places where you needed to be protected but weren't. Notice the ways you needed to be nurtured but weren't. This work takes courage, sis. So invite God to be with you in it. Take your time. Grieve the real losses you endured. While this hard work seems like an unlikely way to healing, I promise you that it's worth it.

You've got to be willing to open your eyes and see the depths of your pain. And I know it's scary. Having eyes to see takes bravery, but I believe in you. I know that if I can do it, you can too. But even more important than my belief, you have a heavenly Father who believes in you—who has not left you. There's a Savior who came down to earth to choose you in spite of you. In spite of your mistakes, your stories of brokenness, and even your greatest sin, He still chooses you.

There's a hard but beautiful story in the Bible that shows a picture of Jesus' desire to choose us no matter what. Jesus was in the temple courts in Jerusalem, which was one of the city's most public places. A lot of religious leaders wanted to silence and arrest Him, but Jesus still showed up, again and again. The scribes and the Pharisees brought a woman who was caught in adultery to the temple courts where Jesus was. I can't help but think about the shame this woman sat in as they chose to bring her to Jesus publicly, when most people who broke the law were kept in custody while their case was discussed. Not to mention the conditions that the woman had to be "caught" in.

According to the law, more than one person had to have witnessed the sexual act, and they had to agree on what they'd seen for the accusation to be taken seriously. There was so much shame and humiliation here for this woman. And there was also a death sentence. Adultery was a capital offense under Jewish law.

Could you imagine being caught in the very act of some of your biggest mistakes, arrested on the spot, and dragged to a public setting to be killed? The mistake you've made that you haven't shared with anyone. The one that is hard to talk about with God or even yourself. That type of shame is what this woman endured publicly, with no forgiveness or second chance in sight. But none of that mattered to the Pharisees. They saw this as an opportunity to force Jesus into breaking the Law of Moses. And their plan was simple: catch this woman in adultery, bring her to a public place where Jesus was teaching and praying, challenge Him by reminding Him that the Law of Moses said that she should be executed for the crime of adultery, and hope they could trap Him. What happened next was both revolutionary and surprising for those at the temple courts that day, and still for us today.

> When they kept on questioning him, he straightened up and said to them, "Let any one of you who is without sin be the first to throw a stone at her." Again he stooped down and wrote on the ground.
>
> At this, those who heard began to go away one at a time, the older ones first, until only Jesus was left, with the woman still standing there. Jesus straightened up and asked her, "Woman, where are they? Has no one condemned you?"
>
> "No one, sir," she said.
>
> "Then neither do I condemn you," Jesus declared. "Go now and leave your life of sin." (John 8:7–11)

You see what just happened there, right?

He flipped the script. Everyone in the temple courts would have been stunned. Anyone who heard His words would have reasoned, *I've committed sin, too, so I guess it wouldn't be right for me to throw a stone at her because the things I've done deserve stones too.*

He chose her over the Law? But she's committed a crime. How could He love someone like her?

Not only did Jesus create accountability for the public shaming, but He also chose to show love to a woman who, to them, was blemished and worthy of death. Her brokenness didn't discount her from access and love from the Savior of the universe. All her deepest regret and pain was on full display, and Jesus didn't shame her about it. Instead, He offered encouragement and next steps. For the Pharisees and religious leaders this was about proving Him wrong, but for Jesus this was about proving His love and loyalty to this woman. This was about choosing the woman over her sin and encouraging her to go and live a life of wholeness and holiness.

When our pain is brought into the light, hope and healing can be found.

Now, don't get me wrong: no one has the right to expose your personal business. And this woman should never have had to endure what she did. But I still think that this moment *when nothing was hidden* was the pivotal moment when her hope and healing began. When we bring our pain into the light, hope and healing are available to us. Maybe you'll decide to tell a trusted friend what happened with that guy you met on Tinder. Or you might decide that it's time to share that one secret you've never uttered with your therapist. Or you might begin by journaling whatever comes up as a way of talking to God and inviting Him into your healing journey. When you decide to bring your hurts into the light, hope and healing can be yours.

You know that woman in the temple courts? Her life isn't so

> **WHEN OUR PAIN IS BROUGHT INTO THE LIGHT, HOPE AND HEALING CAN BE FOUND.**

different from the lives you and I are living. And Jesus *chose* her. He *loved* her. Not only did He choose the woman in the temple courts that day, but He chose you. And me. Jesus knew we'd be here in this moment debating our worth, fighting for healing, and deciding to name even the hard things. Through this act of choosing the woman in John 8, He is showing us today that He chooses you and me as well. Jesus is choosing you right now. The question is, will you be brave enough to fight for your greatest hope by fighting through your greatest hurt? I hope you will. You've come this far. You don't have to allow the voices of insecurity and doubt and shame to keep you hiding from your past. You can absolutely look at all your past mistakes, your past pain, and the parts of your story that you just want to forget and declare that they don't get to have the final say in your life.

JESUS IS CHOOSING YOU RIGHT NOW.

While we don't know this woman's entire backstory, I can relate to her wounds. We don't know why she chose to sleep with a man she wasn't married to, but often these choices come from a place of deep insecurity. From believing that we're not worthy of a deep intentional love that goes far beyond sexual pleasure. And we don't even know that the choice was hers! In a strongly patriarchal culture, she may have been coerced. If she used sex to soothe the pain inside, I get it. I'd used alcohol, drugs, and partying to numb the deepest wounds of my childhood and the bad decisions I made thereafter. I was in a spiral of wounds and numbing. I felt like I had no way out. And I believed if I dared go to Jesus, He would have more shame and disappointment for me. Or worse, He would be unaware that I was drowning in this spiral because He'd totally forgotten about me.

We all have things we need to heal from. Whether it's sexual abuse, bullying, church hurt, divorce, parental trauma, the list goes on. We all have things that have deeply hurt us. We need restoration and true freedom. Our childhood wounds can be transformed into adult scars that are healed and sealed.

> OUR CHILDHOOD WOUNDS CAN BE TRANSFORMED INTO ADULT SCARS THAT ARE HEALED AND SEALED.

And our unhealed places aren't contained. Whether we like it or not, unhealth and trauma leak. We aren't just unhealthy women or wives or moms, but the unhealth spills out into our work, our friendships, and even our relationship with God. If you want to move forward into a place of hope, you're going to have to fight for it. And the first place you can start fighting is with your words. So remember: when you name the source of your brokenness, healing begins.

CHAPTER 3

BROKEN CRAYONS STILL COLOR

I FOUND HOPE AND YOU CAN TOO

I carried my childhood wounds and destructive teen behavior into college with me—partying and drinking and looking for that same validation in men. After college I moved to a different state to live with a man I'd dated for only three months. I was nineteen when we got engaged, and we married soon after. I thought I'd spend the rest of my life with him, but our arguments turned to rage, doors hanging off hinges, and holes in walls. And a daughter was born into all that toxicity.

And while it is heartbreaking to have endured a hard childhood that was followed by difficult teenage years, then even more excruciating young-adult years, all before twenty-five, it's my story. And maybe it's what your story feels like. One bad thing after another. One bad relationship after another. One toxic environment after the next. Well, here's the good news: it did get better for me. But the healing required real work, intentionality, and the most important relationship I'd ever form: my relationship with Jesus.

I wanted to be a healthier, more whole, and a holier Toni. I deserved that, and so did my family. It really is true that when we experience trauma, we leak. And pain and unhealthy coping doesn't isolate itself to just one area of life. If you're an unhealthy person, you're an unhealthy mom, daughter, friend, wife, girlfriend, and leader. I wanted to be healthy, and I needed Jesus to get me there. But how?

My friend-turned-coach Erica led me in a session where we created a life plan for me that helped bring clarity to my God-given purpose. And part of the plan was to attend something called a "spiritual encounter" known as Feminine Hearts Alive. It was a getaway for women who wanted to learn how to hear from God. A lovely couple ran it every year in Georgia, believing that women would come fully alive to their God-given feminine hearts in a way that only God could activate. Erica had experienced it, and she described it as one of the most healing experiences she'd ever had. She went on and on about how life-changing it was, how I'd be close to God like never before, and even how I'd learn to hear the voice of God. Sis, she really sold this thing. And I was in! At the end of the life-planning session with Erica, I rolled up the extra-large, Super Sticky Easel Sheets with my life plan written out on them, tucked them under my arm, and went home to sign up for the spiritual encounter where I'd learn how to become closer to and hear the voice of God.

I wanted to hear it. After all, I'd lived all these years with different views of God based on what people told me. I figured if He could just tell me Himself, I'd be a lot better off. Especially because while growing up I'd learned that He was this big, mean God who was shaking His finger at me, scolding me for all I had done. And then as an adult I believed my first pastor when he made it seem like God asks us to serve tirelessly at church, as directed, without question or boundaries. I believed that God never came to my rescue when I felt all alone taking care of my mom, processing sexual manipulation, and numbing with alcohol and drugs. He didn't protect me, and He was ashamed of me. God only wanted to get close to me when I was perfect. I needed to hear what He thought of me because for some reason I didn't believe all I'd been told.

After finding a new, healthier church home, North Point Community Church, before doing the life plan, I'd started to believe that God was gentle and kind. The words my new pastor used were the complete opposite of what I'd grown up hearing in church and definitely different from what I'd heard in the church where I'd been saved at age twenty-one. So, feeling confused and determined to get God to prove who He was, I signed up for the spiritual encounter.

One week before the encounter, however, something interesting happened. A consulting client told me about a church that helped people hear from God. Being the extroverted, determined-to-hear-from-God person that I was, a few days later I showed up there and sat on the very back row. You know, the row that's not a row in the back of the sanctuary? The one that's essentially chairs lined up on the back wall? That one. I'd done some research, and Grace Church was the real deal. I checked out the testimonies on their website. I Insta-stalked them on their Instagram page. I even knew a friend who'd attended, and her life was changed forever. They believed and practiced healing people from sicknesses and prophetically speaking about things that God was doing in the lives of His sons and daughters. I was a little intimidated and prayed that I could just coast in the back without anyone asking me questions or talking to me.

The service went well. Worship, LED lights, a host, and some fun announcements. It was church. But then a pastor started praying, and in the middle of her prayer, she turned to everyone and addressed the congregation.

She said, "I believe the Lord is calling this entire room to pray for one another. And if you have a prophetic word that God has placed on the inside of you to speak to someone else, please at this time say it."

I didn't think anyone would notice me, but lo and behold an older gentleman came by and said, "Hi, my name is Robert. I'd love to pray with you."

Robert and I prayed, and midway through the prayer he asked God for a prophetic word for me but didn't share that he'd received one.

We opened our eyes and Robert asked, "Would you like to say anything to me from God?"

I hadn't thought to ask God for anything during our prayer, and as far as I could tell He wasn't speaking to me.

I gently stuttered, "Umm, God is saying He's proud of you and close to umm your heart." Those were the only words that came to my mind in the moment. And while not 100 percent confident they were from God, I believed that about God.

He smiled.

Then proceeded to tell me what he was sensing from God for me.

"I believe God is saying that a new season is ahead. A deeper season, one of much discovery for you. I also believe that God is leading you to read the psalm of your birthday year. When were you born?"

"1991," I said, my eyebrows furrowed.

He finished by saying, "That's great. You should read Psalm 91. It'll be very important."

I thanked him, the service finished, and I rushed home, obviously, to read Psalm 91. I parked, hopped out, closed my car door, and Olympic power-walked through the garage, down the hallway, flung open my door, and headed to my couch. I dusted off my Bible, flipped those little pages to Psalms, and there it was. Psalm 91! I read each line carefully. Words like: "You'll stand untouched, watch it all from a distance, watch the wicked turn into corpses." And "You'll walk unharmed among lions and snakes, and kick young lions and serpents from the path" (vv. 8, 13 THE MESSAGE). It literally meant nothing to me! Not kidding. I didn't resonate with anything it said. My first thought was, *Well, that guy was really off.*

I was sad but still determined to attend the spiritual encounter and maybe hear God for myself there. I'd discounted God and who He was based on my circumstances, not based on what Jesus had done on the cross for me. I wasn't going back to that. I couldn't allow an experience with my first pastor, a deeply flawed person, to write a story in my heart about a perfect Savior. A Savior who is so unlike people in this world. I'd done that before. I believed there was a better way to the life I wanted, and I would stop at nothing to go get it.

As I drove down from north Georgia where I lived to south Georgia where the spiritual encounter was going to be, I remember playing worship music but not singing along or really listening to it. I think I knew the motions of being "spiritual," but I couldn't find the words or strategies to prepare for what I wanted to receive at this encounter. So I just listened to the lyrics and drove until I pulled onto a winding dirt road, passing deer and trees that had welcomed many women to this holy place for many decades. When I reached the driveway, I turned the worship music down and the staff greeted me. They asked for my name and if they could take my bags to my cabin for me. I was already being lavished with hospitality and cared for. My shoulders dropped and my tongue released from the roof of my mouth. I was ready.

I walked into the spiritual encounter expecting the God of the universe to meet me there. About seventy-five other women and I arrived at a breathtaking retreat center with white clay-styled cottages laced with red brick and topped with castle-turret roofing. These buildings looked like beautiful white cylinders with red birthday hats on, waiting to celebrate a group of hesitant but spiritually desperate women. I sat in each group session in a small cathedral-style sanctuary and learned about how God had uniquely made me as a woman. I learned about how He was captivated by my beautiful heart. I learned that after God created the moon and the earth and the stars and even man, He wasn't finished until He created you and me—woman. I marveled at being called "the *period* to earth's creation." I wept silently when I realized that we are the final stroke to God's masterpiece that is the world.

I even learned to identify the deepest lie I'd believed. Because I was unsafe and unprotected, the Enemy had hissed to my heart, "No one will come to rescue you." As a little girl I'd been alone, fending off harm and caring for my mom. And the Holy Spirit revealed that God had been protecting me the whole time. It was such a breath of fresh air for my soul. Over the course of the encounter, I learned how to have intentional quiet time with God and ask Him intimate questions, then pause to hear and feel the impressions He was placing on my heart.

One of the things God kept showing me during our scheduled quiet times was a vision of me in the middle of a field. Every time I closed my eyes, there I was. In the middle of a field with my arms stretched out wide, twirling around. My chin was tilted up, my eyes were closed, and my arms flailed as I spun around and around. Then, as I watched myself, I noticed a lion in the field about sixty yards away from me. But strangely it couldn't get to me, and I wasn't even afraid of it. I wrote down that vision in my journal and kept pursuing God's voice. I used the journal prompts the encounter team taught us, and they started to work. I could feel God so close to me. The words in my journal went from just a few on the first and second days to pages of things God was speaking to my heart on the third and fourth days. I was pursuing God with an open heart, and He was pursuing me right back.

After four days together that felt like two weeks, we ended our time. As I drove back home, I felt changed. I knew deep in my soul that God was with me, protecting me, looking after me. This was more than just figuring out my gifts, talents, and purpose on sticky pads during a life-planning session. This was a drastic change in my soul. I felt God's presence because I had invited Him in. I began to walk with a type of daughterly pride because I knew my heavenly Father was with me. I felt renewed in who I was in God. The next morning I woke up, sat on my couch, and began my quiet time. I used a quiet-time strategy called 7–4–1 that I'd learned at the encounter. (We'll unpack that later in the book.) At the very end of my quiet time, I asked God, "What scripture are You leading me to today?"

Psalm 91, I heard Him say. "I'm sorry, what? Psalm 91? The scripture the guy gave me? The one that meant nothing to me? God, are You sure?" I closed my eyes and prayed again asking what scripture God was leading me to for the day. And clearly, I felt He was leading me right back to Psalm 91. I rolled my eyes, opened my Bible where the ribbon was still draped inside Psalm 91, and read.

> You who sit down in the High God's presence,
> spend the night in Shaddai's shadow,
> Say this: "GOD, you're my refuge.
> I trust in you and I'm safe!"
> That's right—he rescues you from hidden traps,
> shields you from deadly hazards.
> His huge outstretched arms protect you—
> under them you're perfectly safe;
> his arms fend off all harm.

I pictured a grandpa holding his little granddaughter making her feel safe and loved.

> Fear nothing—not wild wolves in the night,
> not flying arrows in the day,
> Not disease that prowls through the darkness,
> not disaster that erupts at high noon.
> Even though others succumb all around,
> drop like flies right and left,
> no harm will even graze you.

You'll stand untouched, watch it all from a distance,
watch the wicked turn into corpses.

My mind couldn't fathom this kind of protection and safety.

Yes, because GOD's your refuge,
the High God your very own home,
Evil can't get close to you,
harm can't get through the door.
He ordered his angels
to guard you wherever you go.
If you stumble, they'll catch you;
their job is to keep you from falling.
You'll walk unharmed among lions and snakes,
and kick young lions and serpents from the path.

(PSALM 91:1–13 THE MESSAGE)

I gasped. *The vision!* The field, me in it flailing my arms, the lion and not being harmed. That deep lie I'd believed, that I was unsafe, flashed into my thoughts. *He was there.* He was showing me everything.

"Evil can't get close to you."

It was all there, and I was freaking out! The writer of this psalm, David, was writing what felt like my story. The lion, the danger, the protection, the safety of my Father in heaven. Everything I had felt and been imagining was right here. I went way past ugly crying to lying prostrate and repeating, "Thank You, God" over and over again. He had been there all along. And even when evil tried to take me out, He was there rescuing me. He was protecting me. He is why I am still standing today.

But that wasn't even the best part of the scripture! I knew I had to finish the rest of Psalm 91. After I blew my nose and wiped off what was left of my eyebrows and mascara that I'd forgotten to take care of from the night before, I opened my Bible up again and read:

> "If you'll hold on to me for dear life," says GOD,
>
> "I'll get you out of any trouble.
>
> I'll give you the best of care
>
> if you'll only get to know and trust me.
>
> Call me and I'll answer, be at your side in bad times;
>
> I'll rescue you, then throw you a party.
>
> I'll give you a long life,
>
> give you a long drink of salvation!"
>
> (PSALM 91:14–16 THE MESSAGE)

God had spoken to me in a way I'd never experienced before. It was so far from being a random coincidence that no one could ever convince me otherwise. The man at the prophetic and healing service was right all along, and God had truly spoken to him on my behalf. Shocker!

The scripture hadn't meant a lot to me when I first read it because of where I was in my healing journey with God. My guard had been up with Him, and understandably so. But it needed to come down so He could pursue me. And maybe you are right there in that place. Longing to hear from God, wanting to be pursued by Him, and needing a way forward on your healing journey. Sis, I'm here to tell you that there is a better way.

There's a better way to be close to God. There's a better way to identify the lies and schemes of the Enemy of your soul. There's a better way to go to God for yourself and not depend on someone else to do it for you. There's a better way to healing and wholeness. And sometimes the better way has been in front of us all along, but has been waiting on our willingness to see it. God is immovable. He's unchanging. We are the variable here. Our circumstances, our willingness, our posture, our desire to pursue Him as He pursues us right back. And He *is* pursuing us, in every moment. But the Enemy of our souls doesn't want us to believe that God is with us. That's the big lie that poisons us all. And I suspect that there's another lie you've believed that's particular to your experience.

THE ENEMY OF OUR SOULS DOESN'T WANT US TO BELIEVE THAT GOD IS WITH US.

Here's what I want to encourage you to start with: name your lie and ask God to show you the truth. Again, when we name our brokenness and boast freely about it, we find freedom in Christ. What did you believe about yourself because of what you experienced early in life? What did that cause you to believe about God? About others? The Enemy seizes what we experienced and uses it to lie to our hearts. He tells us things that aren't true about how God made us. He whispers sentences of defeat into our ears so we'll give up on the chance to be healed from the very things that break us. He'll attempt to confuse us about who we are, our purpose and gifts and talents. And while the lie we believed might seem to be something easy to address with a one-time fix, it takes real intentionality and vulnerability to name the lies that the Enemy has planted deeply in our hearts through the pain of our stories. It takes bravery and courage to do that.

What's your lie? What is the thing that keeps you hidden, separated from God, and in cycles of despair? And what intimate questions can you ask God about this lie?

During the difficult time of my separation from my first husband, maybe three years before the spiritual encounter, I always looked forward to picking up Dylan from preschool. I'd walk down hallways lined with the "art" that sweet little students had made and that would eventually end up on refrigerators. I'd get to Dylan's classroom door, open it, and just like an excited puppy when its owners come home, she would waddle toward me, wrap her little arms around my legs, and power up like a Pokémon. She'd scream, "Mommy!" at the top of her lungs like she hadn't just seen me three hours ago.

Picking up Dylan from preschool was a refuge during that season. After I decided to find safety and wholeness by ending my toxic marriage and fighting through the anxiety of figuring out what life would look like as a single mother, Dylan was the one good thing I still had. And picking her up from school was almost always the most joyful part of my week. We had a long journey ahead. One

WHEN WE NAME OUR BROKENNESS AND BOAST FREELY ABOUT IT, WE FIND FREEDOM IN CHRIST.

of rebuilding and starting over. I didn't know where hope was going to come from, but I knew I had a little girl who needed me to find it.

One day I parked my car, walked through the parking lot, and walked down the hallway wearing my mom jeans. I was doing my usual thing. Then I got to Dylan's classroom door, opened it—and no Dylan. No waddling, no yelling my name, nothing. My expression must've been a sad sight because when her teacher and I locked eyes, she immediately rushed over to me and said, "Dylan is fine!"

I took a deep breath. My anxiety and PTSD after so much fear and so many years of fighting had made me jump to the worst-case scenario—that someone had hurt her, or something had gone badly.

The teacher explained, "We brought out a new art kit today in class and Dylan absolutely loved it. She's been in the corner coloring and drawing all day."

My eyes lit up. I thought, *My kid is going to be the next Picasso. She's going to be a professional artist and she's probably going to take her mom to Paris. I need to get on Amazon and order a beret and a faux fur.*

As an Enneagram three, an achiever who always wants to crush it every single day, I got so excited. And a part of me needed this. Walking through a failed and toxic marriage, attending a spiritually abusive church, and remembering the days when I felt as if my parents didn't champion my efforts as a kid, I wanted to show Dylan something different. And maybe we'd find a little hope in doing something fun like coloring and painting. Creating something beautiful when everything around us seemed so dark.

Next thing you know Dylan and I were in Target (said with a French accent because, you know, Paris). I somehow managed to get an easel in the cart. The one with the dry erase on one side and the chalkboard on the other. I also squeezed an entire craft paper easel roll into the cart. Per Dylan's request, I threw in an Elsa from *Frozen* coloring book. Then, when I hit the Crayola aisle, something magical happened. It was like I was reliving my childhood.

As we were rolling down aisle seven inch by inch, I stopped at the Holy Grail of coloring: the sixty-four box of crayons. This was a national treasure in my childhood. Where there's now an iPad and a stylus in my kid's hand, there was a sixty-four box and sharpener in mine years ago. Wide-eyed, hands shaking, I grabbed the box and tucked it under my arm.

With not a lot of money in my single-mom bank account, I

checked out at Target whispering a silent prayer that my payment would be accepted and I wouldn't have to feel the embarrassment of a denied card. It went through. When we got home, I set up Dylan in our living room with her easel, canvas paper, coloring pages, and the beloved sixty-four box of crayons.

I looked in her little eyes and said, "Let God use you. Create freely. And remember, Paris is waiting on us."

I headed into the kitchen to cook her favorite meal, "pasghetti." I was sure this would stir up some creativity. Plus, spaghetti was one of those foods that would last us a few days so we could stay within budget as I strategically planned to have coffee for breakfast and lunch for the rest of the week while filling up on spaghetti for dinner.

After cooking, I slowly walked into the living room. All over the floor in mini piles were crayons that looked like they'd gotten into a fight. Dylan had robbed these crayons of their dignity. They were naked, and their little clothes were peeled off. And when I looked to my left (because I saw something dark in my peripheral vision), there was a mural on the wall of some sort. Dylan had taken a crayon, waddled over to the wall, and completely "Picassoed" the bottom half of it.

I looked over at Dylan. She was lying on her stomach as if nothing had happened. And when I asked why she'd ruined all the crayons, she just looked at me with all her sass and said, "Mommy, color." And then looked back at her drawing.

After putting her to bed, I walked downstairs to clean up everything, regretting, once again, that I didn't have anyone around to help. And as I was on my knees scraping up the crayons, while the thickness of the carpet was flipping them over my hands, I had a breakdown. My plan to bring a little hope into our broken home ended just as quickly as it began.

The truth was, I was exhausted, alone, and in tears. This wasn't about crayons; it was about a life that had come crashing down into broken pieces of despair. And at twenty-five years old I felt like a complete mess. Broken, like the crayons scattered on our carpet. I'd spent countless nights shuffling through divorce papers because I couldn't afford a lawyer. I'd looked at my finances, my unemployment check, and the bills I would now be carrying as a single mom. Dylan and I would eventually have to move into an apartment with a friend—a fellow single mom—and her daughter.

I was wrestling with the decision to allow my parents to keep Dylan over the summer months for "grandparents camp" while I got myself together. I'd been fired from a church that had promised me a promotion and raise a few months before they let me go. I felt hopeless and disqualified because of my brokenness. I was in a valley of complete darkness, and I just didn't see a way to claw my daughter and myself out of it.

I thought back to the mess of broken crayons on the floor and Dylan's comment to me: "Mommy, color." With her childlike resilience, I realized that she was saying, "Yeah, I broke the crayons, Mom, but they still work!" They weren't broken to depletion in her little mind. They were still working, still capable, still worthy.

I found hope, and it's available to you too. I found the same resilience Dylan offered up about a broken crayon, but about my life. My brokenness didn't stand a chance against my willingness to fight for my healing with grit and holy pursuit. Resurrection in our lives is a powerful thing when we recognize that resurrection has no power without death, without picking up the broken pieces of our stories and realizing that they're still capable, still able to be used.

A real encounter with God made me realize that God was willing to help me become a healthier, more whole, and even holier Toni. I know that because He did it. He gave me a road map to healing and wholeness. He gave me a better way. And He's giving it to you too. It's not at all a coincidence that you're reading this book. It's evidence of God's pursuit of your heart and soul.

You are reading the story of a little girl from Houston, Texas, raised in a blended family with an ill mom; the story of a girl who twerked at parties, drinking until she couldn't remember the party, who turned into a believer in Jesus, finally hearing the voice of God because of a random man at a church service and a spiritual encounter she attended. She founded a women's ministry centered around healing and wholeness.

And then there's *you*. You picked up this book, started reading, and got to this moment. Maybe for the first time you read a story about the God of the universe speaking clearly to a broken but hopeful woman. And that woman, Toni Collier, wants you to know that same God, who wants to speak to you too.

He's gazing at you, sis. And He's waiting for you to return His gaze. God sees you, and He hears your pain. Let's continue this journey and see what fields He wants to meet you in and what dangers He wants to save you from.

CHAPTER 4

HOPE FOR THE HURTING

GOD SEES AND HEARS YOUR PAIN

After we moved in with my single-mom friend and her daughter, Dylan spent that summer staying with my parents for "grandparents camp." During that time I worked two jobs, got connected to a healthy church, and let go of some friends who couldn't hold the pain I was in. Then I started surrounding myself with healthy people as I did the hard work of healing. I went to counseling every week, where I started EMDR trauma treatment (eye movement desensitization and reprocessing) for the deep childhood wounds that needed professional help. I forced myself to attend a sixteen-week trauma group. I read and studied parenting strategies so I could become the parent to Dylan that I wish I'd had. I practiced gratitude for the little things, like not having to eat spaghetti four days in a row because I could finally afford chicken, thanks to my new job at a national nonprofit and being contracted to speak to the youth at my new church. Most important, I dove headfirst into a consistent and personal relationship with Jesus. I found hope in the middle of my greatest hurts until those hurts slowly turned to joy.

I stopped numbing the pain and allowed myself to feel. For the first twenty-five years of my life, I thought that if I just ignored the abuse and trauma and brokenness it would go away. But I was lying to myself. The only real way to freedom and hope, and access to the power of God, was to embrace my brokenness and the painful parts of my story. And when I finally allowed myself to be weak, cracked like the broken vessel I was, God's light began to stream in.

Maybe you want to find hope and joy in the midst of your

deepest hurts too. Maybe you're in a valley right now. Maybe that's why you picked up this book and made it this far. Maybe your brokenness feels big and you're ready to claw your way out. I'm ready for that for you too. Or maybe you've been in hiding because you feel like your brokenness is too small to be considered valid. If that's you, I want to encourage you to honor your pain. Avoid the comparison trap and acknowledge that your pain, big or small, is valid. But it also doesn't have to have the final say in your life. I want to validate whatever valley you're in.

> **AVOID THE COMPARISON TRAP AND ACKNOWLEDGE THAT YOUR PAIN, BIG OR SMALL, IS VALID.**

And I also want to speak to the darkness that has been covering your light by saying this again: *hope is available to you.* Even in my hopelessness and despair, by the power of God and safe community and professional counsel, I discovered a way out. I know it feels like that valley is just too incredibly deep to fight your way to hope, but you can do it. And you can do it because it's not your strength alone that will get you there. God has strength for His people, and He's proved it through the generations.

God does his best work in brokenness. He will find you in the depths of your pain and hurt and He'll give you hope. He'll give you joy. He will give you refuge. But He is not going to force His way into those tender places. You have to make the choice to surrender to Him. You have to lay it all at His feet. You have to be willing to say, "God, help me. I'm at the end. I don't have anything left to give. I need Your strength. I need You to rescue me."

THE ROAD MAP FOR THE BROKEN CRAYONS COMMUNITY

I knew I couldn't let this profound moment I'd had with Dylan and a sixty-four box of crayons be a story just for myself. Out of my story of brokenness and my willingness to press into pain and fight for hope, I created Broken Crayons Still Color, a women's organization that helps walk with women through their stories of abuse, pain, trauma, divorce, anxiety, and so much more. My team and I have created an entire roadmap to help women find hope again. We've walked through this journey ourselves and with women all over the world for eight months at a time, teaching them what we've discovered step-by-step. And while I am not living a perfect life, I know that I am living a redeemed one. I know that while God never promised us a life of perfection, He did promise to be with us in the imperfection. And I can boldly proclaim that I have seen Him be the light guiding my feet in dark valleys. The same is available to you.

Do you remember the verse where the apostle Paul boasted about his weaknesses? I want to circle back to that to offer some words of truth and encouragement from the apostle Paul's letter to the church in Corinth that he'd planted. Remember, during Paul's teaching about boasting he begins to go down a list of all the things *he* could be boastful about—from being beaten for the gospel, to being shipwrecked and in dangerous situations, to being sleep deprived and experiencing deep hunger. Paul, in this context, had a reason to boast about all he'd done to spread the gospel. But instead, he pointed out his weaknesses—his brokenness. And he did it for a very specific reason, one that I think continues to help us today. Paul wrote, "But he said to me, 'My grace is sufficient for you, for my power is made perfect in weakness.' Therefore I will boast all the more gladly about my weaknesses, so that Christ's power may rest on me" (2 Corinthians 12:9).

We're going to break this scripture down. It's important to fully understand what God is trying to say to us and what we get to do about it today. The first part of this scripture is God speaking directly to Paul about a weakness and hardships he faced. I love that God spoke directly and personally to Paul in this scripture. God reminded him that He had grace and it was sufficient for even Paul's brokenness. And I believe that God has grace that's sufficient for us too. I believe He knew we'd be tempted to look to our left and right at everyone else's social media timelines and stories and compare our brokenness. And in that comparison we would be left ashamed of what is in our stories. Then we'd begin to fall into a comparison trap that leads us to pride, boasting about material things that make us look more perfect and hiding the things that don't.

God was saying to us, "Daughter, My grace is sufficient for your mess, your story, your brokenness, all your crazy days and destructive moments. I've got grace for you." And not only that, but when we come out of hiding and become honest and boast about the very things that make us weak, it is traded for God's divine power.

When we boast about our brokenness, Christ's power rests on us. This scripture challenges us to combat some of the lies the world tries to plant in our hearts. And don't those lies seem so real to our hearts and minds?

I have to be perfect to be used by God.
I'm not worthy of healing.
I deserved the pain I've been through.
It would be better if I suffered alone.

If I want to be successful, I can't be honest about my pain.
I have to hide what I endured.
If they find out, I'll be rejected.
God can use others who are broken, but God can't use me.
I'm too broken.

These aren't just thoughts that stay isolated in our heads, but seeds that get deeply rooted in our identities and cause damage that can impact our feelings and actions. But I am inviting you to proclaim, "I won't boast about what I have. I won't boast about how I almost got my eyebrows to look like sisters and not cousins. I won't boast about how much I can do and how well I can speak or preach or teach. Instead, I'm going to boast about my weaknesses. I'm going to be honest about how damaging my childhood was and how ashamed I feel about my divorce. I'm going to be honest about what I'm struggling with. I'm going to invite God into the depths of my pain. I'm going to show up to counseling and be 100 percent real about what I'm feeling. I'm going to be vulnerable and transparent with my safe people!"

Because when we do *that*, Christ's power can and will rest on us.

I want to remind you of four words before you dive into the next chapters. It's what I think my daughter Dylan was trying to say when she broke all those crayons and possibly what God was trying to teach me through her. These four words have changed my life forever: *broken crayons still color.*

Those four words have been a reminder to me that despite everything I've been through, the decisions that I've made or been forced to make, God still wants to use me to create beautiful things in this world and to live a hope-filled life with my scars in tow. There's no brokenness God can't redeem, and there's no darkness that's stronger than the light of Jesus. And not only is hope available to you in your healing, but there's an even more beautiful story to be created using all that brokenness.

Paul taught us this. The thorn in his side he mentioned in 2 Corinthians 12:7, the one he pleaded to be taken away, was the very thing that drove him to boast about his weakness, which then drove God to intervene by infusing Paul with His power. I don't know what you've been taught about God. I don't know if you've heard that He's a big, mean God at the end of the tunnel saying, "Come on, get stronger and all cleaned up and I'll be waiting on you when you get it right." But He is not. His Word is the lamp to your feet and a light to your path (Psalm 119:105). He's not waiting on you to be perfect; He is with you in the imperfect. He's the player on the sidelines yelling, "Put Me in, coach! I've got some strength for your weakness, some power for your brokenness. Put Me in!"

THERE'S NO BROKENNESS GOD CAN'T REDEEM, AND THERE'S NO DARKNESS THAT'S STRONGER THAN THE LIGHT OF JESUS.

In the next few chapters, you will learn about the roadmap our ministry has created for women looking for hope and learning how to live a life of wholeness and healing. We'll walk through how to create a consistent life of prayer and worship with the Lover of your soul, Jesus. We'll also review what it looks like to create safe community around you as you journey toward hope, and what it looks like to transition a toxic community into less intimate places in your life. We'll talk through counseling, what it is and isn't, and how you can engage in the practice of being intentional about your healing. Finally, we'll talk about living a life of gratitude. While gratefulness sounds like a simple task, it can be difficult to look at the good parts of our stories when so much of them feels dark. Along with learning these strategies, there will be opportunities for you to put them into practice and create new consistencies in your story.

I believe with all my heart that it will be a beautiful journey.

PART 2

A ROAD MAP TO HEALING AND HOPE

In part 2, you'll get to learn from the road map that my team and I have put together for you to process through your brokenness and get on the other side to hope. You'll begin to look intently at your faith and learn even more about a God who pursues you and wants to spend time with you. We'll talk about embracing and identifying a healthy and toxic community. We'll even discuss how you can identify your counseling needs and next steps to doing it well.

SURRENDER

BEGINNING YOUR HEALING JOURNEY TO A HOPE-FILLED LIFE

A young mentee of mine, whom I'll call Rena, had a hard time in the boy department. Her father hadn't been present in her life, and she was hurting. Much like many young ladies with daddy wounds, she longed for validation and attention from boys and just didn't care what it looked like. I walked with her mom as she navigated Rena's tough middle school years when her hurt and abandonment turned into anger and rebellion.

After we got through that, I walked with them through her high school years, and we watched something special—we saw healing take place. She began to join extracurricular activities and make friends, and her relationship with her mom got even better. That is, until she got suspended after getting caught skipping class with a boy. Thankfully we made it through that, and she got to college. Her story began to blossom again—that is, until the boyfriend she trusted became sexually aggressive toward her and forced her to do things she didn't want to do. I remember sitting with Rena while tears of shame and embarrassment flowed from her tender heart. She'd been healing, but this was a major setback. And the truth is, that's many of our stories. A trajectory of healing—and then something triggers us.

I've never seen a healing journey that has unfolded in a linear way. And I've never seen one that doesn't include pain and deep sorrow. I know, I know; that escalated pretty quickly. I feel like when we talk about healing, especially in the church, we talk of the light and hopeful days ahead. We talk about God turning our mourning into dancing (Psalm 30:11), but often we forget the in-between. We forget the journey. And while I can confidently say that there is light at the end of the tunnel and there is healing available to you, I would be misleading you if I didn't address the beginning and in-between of that journey.

I'VE NEVER SEEN A HEALING JOURNEY THAT HAS UNFOLDED IN A LINEAR WAY.

"In this world you will have trouble. But take heart! I have overcome the world" (John 16:33). If this isn't one of the most straightforward verses in the Bible, I don't know what is. Jesus is reminding us of what I want to be honest about with you. You will have trouble. It will not be easy. But God, through His Son, Jesus, came before us and conquered the world—and He even left us a Comforter in the Holy Spirit to walk with us through our healing journeys.

BE INTENTIONAL

As we journey together from brokenness and despair to healing and wholeness, there are a few tips I want to give you before diving in. First, I want to encourage you to be focused and intentional about how, when, and where you process this. I would love for you to try to limit distractions and give this your full attention. Your hope is serious, and I don't want you to miss out on what could change the trajectory of your life—not only for you, but for the people you're in relationship with and the generations that may come after you. Can you wake up a little earlier to process through a chapter or two of this book alone? Is there a spot that could be consistently used as a "healing journey" spot in your home? Will you pour yourself a hot drink and make this a moment in your day? Be intentional about the journey, and you'll see rewards.

FIND ACCOUNTABILITY

The next thing I want to encourage you to find is accountability. Often when we begin to look back at our healing journeys and examine the very painful parts, we want to stuff it all back into the places we've used as numbing containers and never face them. But if you have someone to cheer you on along the way and remind you when it gets tough that there's hope waiting for you, it could make all the difference. Most women are verbal processors, so often our answers come after talking our way through a conversation. We'll talk about healthy community in the coming chapters, but if you have safe people in your life now, utilize them. Verbally process with them. If you have a counselor already, it may be a good idea to make him or her aware that you're going through this book and may be triggered by some of the things that come up in your heart.

TAKE YOUR TIME

Go at your own pace. This race most definitely isn't a sprint; it's a marathon. Maybe the most important one you'll ever run or walk. We are all different, we all handle things in different ways, and I want you to stay true to what you need during your journey. We're anti-comparison here, and I believe one of the most freeing things you can do is to own your pace. Fast, slow, pitstops and pauses, whatever you need to get to hope, go for it.

USE A JOURNAL

Use a journal as you read, and write out what you've been learning. You will be a different you in a year, six months, or even just a few weeks. The power of arriving is in being able to look back at where you came from. So journal your journey. And don't forget to look back on it. You're already different now than when you started reading this book because your brain has already begun processing that you can live a more hopeful life. Your heart has begun to recognize that healing and wholeness are available to you. Let's create something beautiful with your brokenness—together.

LET'S GO

Let's talk about my college days. My armpits are sweating already thinking about how vulnerable I'm about to get with you. Those were wild days—let me just say that. I remember being in college at Sam Houston State University as a freshman when my friends and I decided we were going to a toga party at a nearby school. I ripped my turquoise sheet off my dorm bed, grabbed some gold sandals and a gold hippie headband, and went to my friend's house to start designing our togas a few hours before it was time to get on the road to make the two-hour drive.

By the time we got to the party we'd had so much to drink that we stumbled, not walked, into it. All I remember today are flashes of the night. I remember feeling wet grass through the sides of my sandals. I remember spotting guys I'd met before and hugging them tightly so that I could press my chest against theirs and maybe gain some attention. I remember dancing by myself, with my arms open wide spinning and spinning around until I got a headache. I remember having a lime green digital camera around my wrist so I could take pictures of the night and have memories. And I remember the green grass on my hands and knees from crawling around on the ground because I wasn't able to stand from being so drunk.

This was one of the many stories that flashed before me while my eyes were closed at a worship service. I was twenty-one and newly married to my first husband, sitting in the church where I'd just gotten saved. We were having a worship night. Thanks to the lyric video, I belted out worship songs I barely knew. But at the end of the service the pastor had asked if anyone needed to come down to the stage and have a moment with God. So there I was, standing at the edge of the stage with both of my hands pressed down into it. My head was hanging between my shoulders, and I was weeping as the worship team sang.

For the first time in my life, I'd surrendered everything over to Jesus and was having an almost out-of-body experience in which I was visualizing every dark moment of my life. And with each flashback I was startled at how it was a miracle that I had survived. For the first time I started to wonder if God was at the parties, in the moments of desperation, protecting me all along. Spoiler alert: He most definitely was. But to believe it, I had to pursue intimacy with Jesus after receiving Him into my heart. I had to dig deep into my relationship with God through intentional prayer and worship to begin the journey of healing from all the dark moments of my life. I had to believe in a Healer before I could be healed. And that's what was happening every moment I stepped into church on Sundays and lifted my hands in worship and surrender to God. But just like with any relationship, it took more than one day to grow it.

The first step in your healing and wholeness journey is not about faith in God that shows up at church, but one that shows up in your bed, on your couch, at work, and in the curled-up-in-a-ball-in-darkness moments. Your believing in a Healer is ground zero, and it's all about prayer and worship. You may have used these words and not even known what they meant. No matter where you fall on the spectrum of understanding prayer and worship, let's relearn it together. Let's approach these topics as children, curious with awe and wonder. Because this truly is the first step to connecting deeply with the God of healing and seeking Him out in faith as you become more whole and hopeful.

I HAD TO BELIEVE IN A HEALER BEFORE I COULD BE HEALED.

Prayer

I went over to a friend's house to congratulate her after finding out she was pregnant. Her daughter burst out of her room and said, "Yay! I prayed for a year for a baby sister and God gave me one!" My daughter overheard, and on the car ride home she asked me, "Mom, if I prayed for a year for a baby sister, will God give me one too?" Her innocence made me think of all my prayers for the things I longed for. I even thought about some of the friends I prayed for during their hardest seasons. For breakthrough, for healing, for restoration in their marriages.

And then I replied, "Well, babe, God wants you to bring all your prayers to Him, big or small. And He loves us so much that He gives us the ones that He knows are good for us and doesn't give us the ones He thinks won't be good for us. God wants nothing more than for you to talk to Him." She smiled, and later in the ride I heard her whispering to God with her eyes closed.

Part of what it means to be broken human beings is the

realization that there's Someone greater than us at work. And when we realize we're not the author and finisher of our stories, we want to connect with the One who is. We want a relationship with the Creator. Not only the One who created the world but the One who knit us together cell by cell in our mothers' wombs. Prayer is how we do that. But often prayer is mistaken as something else.

- **Prayer is not a magic formula.** It's not intended to be done and then, *poof*, everything we want or don't want will magically appear or disappear.
- **Prayer is not our duty to God.** It's not something that can be checked off a list. As an achiever on the Enneagram personality spectrum, this has been my greatest struggle. I want to perform my way through life. I can attempt to place my value in how much can get done, and I have to be actively aware that I tend to do that with prayer as well.
- **Prayer is not meditation.** There's nothing wrong with meditation. It can bring real peace and rest to our bodies. But prayer is much more than that. Prayer is about connecting to the Source of everlasting life, joy, and purpose. It is very intimate and personal and can simply be a message to God that you love Him and are grateful for everything He's given to you.

Prayer is communicating with God and doesn't require a strategy or a set of rules to follow. I believe that often we focus on the quantity of our prayers when we should be focused on the quality. God wants us to show up as our authentic selves. While He knows everything, He delights in hearing about the things in our lives that scare us and confuse us. That could look like you journaling your honest and raw feelings to God. Pray an honest prayer and tell Him all about it. He can handle it. He looks forward to hearing our deepest desires and requests. He marvels at the beauty of our feminine hearts that become completely surrendered and willing to be held in His hands.

Jesus said, "When you pray, do not be like the hypocrites, for they love to pray standing in the synagogues and on the street corners to be seen by others. Truly I tell you, they have received their reward in full. But when you pray, go into your room, close the door and pray to your Father, who is unseen. Then your Father, who sees what is done in secret, will reward you" (Matthew 6:5–6).

God wants us to pray to Him in intimate spaces with sincere hearts. It is a spiritual breathing of the soul. And just like we feel more connected to our friends when we share our deepest thoughts, feelings, and experiences, when we do that with God, we become more connected to Him.

Worship

I have a friend named Laura who designs and sells beautiful rugs. They are stunning! She also creates beautiful art pieces and has an amazing business doing the thing she loves: creating beautiful long-lasting things for people. I remember her sharing with a group of friends and me how close she feels to God when she's in her studio. I asked her why, and she said, "Well, because it's my form of worship." It was beautiful to hear her talk about how she feels closer to God when she's in the studio using her hands to create beautiful things and listening to worship music. We sometimes think of worship as simply singing a song and lifting our hands at church, but worship is in every moment we unplug from the chaos around us and connect to God.

Worship is our intense adoration of God. It's an act of giving thanks to God and an expression of our deep gratitude as an outcome of our prayers to Him. Our worship is our reverence to God and can be done through singing, dancing, and even chanting in God's presence. Our worship can show up in different ways because it is our response to His goodness. Maybe someone in your family was healed from an illness. Our response of deep gratitude and thanks is worship. It is simply our way of honoring Him because He deserves it.

Prayer and worship are critical to our journey here on earth, and I believe they're very important to our healing and wholeness journey as well. Paul the apostle wrote, "Pray without ceasing . . . for this is the will of God in Christ Jesus concerning you" (1 Thessalonians 5:17, 18 KJV). Not only was Paul urging us to pray, but we are directed to pray without ceasing. Relentlessly—about all things for all reasons, and with faith and belief that God is on the throne and can do all things according to His will. Through my own stories of abuse, pain, manipulation, and trauma, I have needed to pray. Not only about the things I've done, but also over my situation and the hardship of it. I've had to pray for healing and strength. And on the other side of my prayers, I've worshipped God for showing up every single time. We are called to pray, and we are called to worship our Creator. God designed us for it. It's built into our very existence. Because we are made in His image, we are to exhibit Christlike behavior. And Jesus prayed without ceasing. By His example, He showed us the importance of it.

Maybe you're a creator, and you'll worship God as you're painting on canvas or strumming strings. Or you might discover that your commute to and from work becomes the perfect time to worship, as your Toyota becomes a sanctuary. Maybe you'll choose to activate your introvert powers and sit in silence, openhanded and openhearted, and just let our Father in. And if you need to do the hard work of setting the alarm thirty minutes early to find time to worship, I promise you that it's worth it. God will meet you there.

THE ENEMY INTERFERES

But the Enemy doesn't want us to pray or worship; he wants us to stay hidden and quiet. Doubt, destruction, misalignment, and confusion are the work of our spiritual Enemy. And when we begin to use our spiritual breath, he goes after it to distract us. He'll do anything to clutter your thoughts and keep you doubting who God is and how powerful your prayer and worship is.

Prayer is necessary for building confidence in God. When you begin to pray for things and God answers them, your confidence in Him grows. And when your confidence grows after answered prayers, you begin to worship Him for what He's done. The more prayers come from you, the more worship comes from you. Your godly confidence—*faith*—grows. And the Enemy doesn't want you to be confident. So he'll whisper lies into your heart to keep you from praying.

If God's truth says He wants to be close to your broken heart (Psalm 34:18), the Enemy will plant the lie that you're too broken to be loved.

If God's truth says that He will rescue you from all harm and you are safe with Him (Psalm 91 THE MESSAGE), the Enemy will plant the lie that you're alone and unprotected.

If God's truth says that He has chosen you for a purpose, on purpose (1 Peter 2:9), the Enemy will plant the lie that says you're unlovable and forgotten.

If God's truth says, Come to Me when you're weary (Matthew 11:28), the Enemy will plant the lie that your burdens are too heavy to carry.

The Enemy's lies sound a lot like God's truth. As my friend Cassandra Speer says, "Thieves don't steal from empty houses." The Enemy is not coming after the things that don't impact you, that don't have substance or meaning to you. He's coming for the truth that you long to hear from God, and he's going to try to dismantle and thwart it enough for you to stop believing God's truth.

I remember seeing this in real time in the life of one of my closest friends, Brittney. After going to the spiritual encounter by myself, I'd decided to take some friends to experience it, including one of my closest friends who isn't in the "professional Christian" bubble like many of my other friends. In fact, Brittney wasn't even the type of girl who attended church regularly. Not because of her lack of faith, but it simply wasn't a part of the routine she and her family had created. After visiting a few churches, they just didn't find a good fit. But after months of my trying to convince her to come on the retreat with me, she gave in and said yes.

THE ENEMY'S LIES SOUND A LOT LIKE GOD'S TRUTH.

I'd told her that the Holy Spirit was all over this place and that she could have a real encounter with God. I don't know if she completely believed me, but she trusted that I wouldn't lead her into something weird. We drove onto the property and unpacked our bags in our assigned rooms with six other women I'd convinced to come. I was over the moon that my friends would get to experience what I had—a real, tangible encounter with the God of the universe.

During the second day of the encounter, the leaders led us through an exercise where we asked God to give us each a brand-new name. A name that would describe how He felt about us, or that was significant for us in this season. We were supposed to spend hours alone praying to God, listening to His voice, and being open to hearing our new names. After that time, our group of eight gathered in our cabin lobby and talked through our names. From biblical names to names of characters in Disney shows, we went one by one, each unpacking the name God had given her. My friend's turn came, and with hesitation and a little confusion she muttered, "I heard the name 'Heather.'" Most of our eyebrows lifted in surprise, and there was a little bit of snickering.

Brittney joked, "I'm a little surprised and doubtful because I only know women with the name Heather who are white. And well . . . you girls know I'm Black through and through. So, I don't know what God is doing here. Maybe I heard it wrong."

Brittney didn't even bother to look up the name Heather to see what meanings it had behind it because she had become convinced that God might not be speaking to her. Before I went to bed that night, I remember praying for her. I whispered, "Lord, You are the author of her story, and I believe in Your plans for her life."

The next day during free time we rented bikes and decided to go on a little ride. Brittney and a few others almost didn't come. They said they weren't "athletic" and couldn't go too far. But in the end, they joined us. We decided to ride down a dirt road to an old school that was long deserted but said to be a beautiful place to see while we were on the property. One pedal after another, with a few stops along the way, we made it. We parked our bikes in a row against the trees and walked up to the school. Although it was locked and we couldn't get in, we dusted off windows with our jackets and peeked in. Little desks and books and dusty chalkboards filled the classrooms. It was beautiful to imagine that decades before we arrived these little chairs were filled with students eager to learn.

Before we left, I spotted Brittney at a window with shock on her face and watery eyes. I walked over to her and asked, "Is everything okay?" She turned to me almost unable to speak as her eyes became too full to contain the tears. She placed her finger on the window, underneath words that had been scratched into it: "Heather was here."

We all burst into childlike squeals. Not only did God give Brittney a new name, but she had had a tangible encounter with Him. She couldn't believe it. There He was, reaching out to her through a name that she didn't think fit her. She'd done the work of praying and sitting with God. She'd asked for God to show her something real. And He had answered!

When we huddled up after the day, Brittney read to us the meaning of the name Heather: "A flowering evergreen plant that thrives on peaty barren lands."[1] This was the name for a resilient flower that could grow despite its rocky, tough surroundings. From her tears and shock, I could tell that worship was going to come from this moment. She expressed to us that she'd always resonated with the description, "the rose that grew from concrete."[2] She'd always felt like she knew she had what it took to live a beautiful, successful life, but that it was never easy; it was always out of really hard circumstances. She'd heard God. He'd connected with the very thing she'd been processing for years. I knew she was going to have a moment of thanksgiving and gratitude with God. Because that's the outcome of answered prayers. A heart of worship to a God who can and will. And you can have that as well.

It's not available just to "professional Christians" or the preachers and teachers; it's for us all. It's for the women who commit to praying and who surrender their praise to a God who deserves it. It's available to you, daughter of the King. So let's go after it. Let's learn how to pray to and worship your Creator. The One who's waiting on you. The One who wants to give you a brand-new name. The One who wants to meet you in the silent moments and show you through miracles, signs, and wonders that you are not alone. Very far from it indeed. Let's unpack practical next steps to living a life that includes consistent prayer and worship.

PRACTICAL PRAYER POINTS

My friend Jennifer and her husband prayed for a baby for more than five years, and it just didn't happen. They prayed at church, prayed with family and friends, and prayed in the secret places alone with God. In their closets, in their bed, eyes closed, lying hand-in-hand. In the places only they knew about. Then they adopted a sweet little girl, and their family felt complete. Two years later the desire returned to have a biological child, and they began praying about it again. One year after that, Jennifer became pregnant with a baby boy. The way their prayers were answered influenced us all. What's beautiful about this story is that their prayers didn't stop. They continued to pray about the future of their family. Their jobs. Their home. Their purpose. They pressed into God, not for the sake of answered prayers but to be close with God in their prayers and whatever the outcome would be. They fully accepted whatever God's will was for them and surrendered their prayers and worship to God. And that type of commitment is inspiring.

How do we take our desires, worries, requests, and words to God and make prayer a part of our daily lives? Any routine we want to create will take intentionality, strategy, and practice. Prayer may be a spiritual action, but it also requires our intellect and our time. I'm excited because I'll be giving you practical tools—strategies I use to help me create a consistent and loving relationship with God. This will be something you can bookmark and come back to if you're struggling with prayer in a future season, or when life gets overwhelming and schedules get hectic and you need to press the reset button on your prayer life. This section isn't about consuming information; it's about deeply learning something that matters to God, to your heart, and on the days when life gets tough. This is about building hope.

When I walk with women through hopelessness—whether it is through my ministry's women's course, the Hopeful Woman Course, or through individual mentorship—and ask them about their prayer lives, they typically say one of two things: "I don't know *how* to pray, Toni." Or, "I don't know *what* to pray about." Often when we've been through painful parts of our story, we become hopeless and lose touch with what our hearts need. Our longings turn into loneliness. Our desires turn into despair. And we sink so deep in a valley, we can't even find the words to pray to help get us through. So we have to identify what prayers our hearts need.

Find Your Secret Place

I want to start this discussion on prayer in the secret place. My public prayers became more powerful when I began saying them more in the secret place. I've found in the past that the prayers I've said from a stage or in church were great, but when I brought them to God alone, it created more space for Him to tend to my heart personally. When I encouraged you to pray, I mentioned a passage from Matthew 6. Let's look at it again as we unpack it. Jesus said:

> When you pray, do not be like the hypocrites, for they love to pray standing in the synagogues and on the street corners to be seen by others. Truly I tell you, they have received their reward in full. But when you pray, go into your room, close the door and pray to your Father, who is unseen. Then your Father, who sees what is

done in secret, will reward you. And when you pray, do not keep on babbling like pagans, for they think they will be heard because of their many words. (Matthew 6:5–7)

God wants to meet with us in secret. He wants it to be just Him and us. He isn't worried about you delivering that Oscar-award-winning prayer speech in front of everyone. In fact, He urges us to let go of the desire for people to look at us when we pray so we can look cool or super-holy.

Find your secret place, and when you do, figure out when you'll go there to meet Jesus. Is it first thing in the morning? Is it right before bed to end the day? Can you take the last half of your lunch break to just sit with God? Take a few moments and think about where and when that might happen.

Now that you have your place, let's talk about what to do when you get there.

The 7–4–1 Prayer

This prayer strategy has truly changed my life. My friends at Feminine Hearts Alive call it the 7–4–1 method. I have used it to help thousands of women around the country kickstart or reignite their prayer lives. The 7–4–1 method challenges you to take seven minutes a day, four days a week, with one day to review and believe what Jesus has been saying to you. Listed below are the seven steps you'll repeat for four days each week. Now, this process may take you longer than seven minutes at the beginning, and that's okay. It's also okay to start by doing the first six steps and adding number seven as you get more comfortable diving into the Bible. This is all just an on-ramp to help you to get into a rhythm and experience what it feels like to have intimate time with God. Then at the end of the week, after you've finished four days (either back-to-back or with a day between), just make sure you have a day left in the week to reflect. You may be a Monday starter like me, or you might want to wait until Wednesday and end on Sunday. Take the time to read over what God has spoken to you. You'll be blown away! It will be glorious! You can even write the words He's spoken to you in a different color or highlight them so you can easily go back to them. It's a great way to capture a summary of all God speaks to you in your time with Him.

The 7–4–1 method has the potential to change absolutely everything when it comes to prayer and worship in your life. It's an incredible framework for intentional time with God if you're just starting out, need to get back into your quiet-time groove, or you're in a season when you don't have a lot of time in your day. Once you're settled into your quiet place, here's how it works:

1. **Close your eyes.** Drop your shoulders, let your tongue fall down from the roof of your mouth, and take a deep breath in for four seconds, hold that breath for four seconds, and then release it for six seconds. Repeat this four times. Deep breath in, hold it, let it go. As you begin your seven minutes, you would write in your journal or notes on your phone or computer as you go to the next steps.

2. **Talk to God.** This may seem silly, but tell Him how you feel. Are you having a good day? Do you feel burdened or light? Are you feeling weary or energetic? Are you optimistic about your day or are you carrying some anxiety into it? God is your heavenly Father and He wants to check in with you and hear how you are.

3. **Reflect on yesterday's emotion.** Take a moment to reflect on any big feelings from the previous day. It's important to take inventory of how something may have affected you and

any big emotions or triggered feelings that came with it. Write that down.

4. **Confess.** I know that word is a little weird. Confession can make us feel unworthy and ashamed of what we've done. But the reality is, confession is telling our stories in truth in a safe environment. God's presence is safe, sis. And when we confess, we not only acknowledge our sins, but we also begin to agree with what God has done with those sins. He sent His Son, Jesus, our big Brother, to give us the freedom to declare that we are forgiven and are no longer bound to sin. Name that sin. Write it out and give it to God to cover.

Now, I understand if this is hard. There have been moments when I've had trouble naming my sin. Not because I've felt ashamed, but because at first I didn't think there was anything to confess. So I asked the Holy Spirit, "Can You reveal some areas in my life that I need to confess?" Almost every time, something came to mind.

5. **Love on God, worshipping Him.** Use what we've been talking about regarding worship. Remember, our worship is our intense adoration of God. It's an act of giving thanks to God and an expression of our deep gratitude as an outcome of our prayers to Him. Tell God how you feel about Him. Think about the times He's shown up for you, protected you, given you a new perspective, restored something. And tell Him how much you appreciate that. Even in the midst of deep sorrow, relationships need tending. And your relationship with God is no different. A simple "thank You for being who You are, totally in control and the Creator of all things good" may be all you have some days.

6. **Invite God to speak to you.** This is one of the most important parts. This may also be the hardest part of this time

with God. Many of us have grown up thinking God either can't speak to us or that He just doesn't want to. I believe He wants nothing more than to speak to our beautiful hearts. God isn't an intruder, but He will be a delightful guest once you invite Him in. This invitation could be written or even said aloud: "Jesus, I want to learn how to hear Your voice. Do You have anything You want to say to me? Do You have any words for me?"

I bet reading those questions, it feels kind of intimate, maybe even childlike. But aren't we supposed to be like children with God? Using a sweet child as an example in Matthew 18:4, Jesus said, "Whoever humbles himself like this child is the greatest in the kingdom of heaven" (ESV). He wants us to be curious and open. He wants awe and wonder to fill our hearts. So ask intimate questions, be curious, and be open to what God can reveal in you. Then listen and write what He tells you. Remember this: anything in your heart that contradicts Scripture is not from God. For example, "I think God is leading me into this affair." Our God's voice is one of peace, kindness, joy, and gentleness. He won't lead you to do harmful things for yourself or for others.

Here are more examples of intimate questions to ask:

- God, would You show me how much You love me? Give me a picture, a memory, a verse that shows me.
- God, what do You think of my heart?
- God, what do You think of my life?
- God, what do You think of me as Your daughter?
- God, do You have a new name for me that shows me or tells me how You see me?
- God, what do You want to say to my broken heart?

7. **Read your Bible.** Wherever you are in your Christian journey, with a new or with a worn-out, highlighted Bible, know
that it is truly a book that anyone can read and be inspired
by. Think about the Bible as a guide to living a life of freedom
and light. Ezekiel 11:19 says, "I'll give you a new heart. I'll put
a new spirit in you. I'll cut out your stone heart and replace
it with a red-blooded, firm muscled heart" (THE MESSAGE).
God's Word gives you a new heart and a new spirit and helps
to renew the hard places in your heart. The Bible shows God's
character and gives us divine revelation of who He has been
and who He is to us. It shows us what God's will is for our
lives, it nourishes our spirits to be alive and awake to who
God is. It teaches us how to live a life of righteousness and
gives us the power to overcome. With each attack by Satan,
Jesus turned to the same place that we can turn to: God's
Word. Maybe the Bible is overwhelming to you, and you just
don't know where to start. That's okay. You can ask God,
"What do You have to say to me through Your Word?" and
wait to find out where you feel most led to read.

Story break: I remember a time when God kept pointing me to
Psalms. It lasted for maybe two months. Every time I would ask what
He wanted me to read, He would place an impression on my heart
to read Psalms. One that caught my attention was Psalm 27. It's a
beautiful scripture all about David's one desire to dwell in the house
of the Lord in the midst of war and darkness. I was on a Zoom call
with the women our ministry gets to serve, and I started sharing this
scripture with the women. A woman with tears in her eyes unmuted
and said, "Toni, on September 3" (she remembered the exact date
because it was the day she was moving), "I just felt God urging me
to pray for you and I kept hearing the word *Psalm* over you."

With tears in my eyes, I hopped out of my chair to grab my journal and flipped fervently to the page of the first day God had told me to read the psalms. You guessed it: September 3. We all gasped, and the awe and wonder of God filled our tender hearts.

Then a second woman unmuted her mic to say, "Psalm 27. It's been my favorite scripture for years. And you speaking that today was just confirmation that God had not forgotten about me. That He was still with me in the wars of life. Thank you."

Cray, right? This is what happens when we allow God into every aspect of our lives. He speaks to us and works for us, and then even through us. We'll talk about that a little later on.

But for now, don't forget this: The Enemy will tempt you to believe that God won't talk to you or that He doesn't want to. Thoughts will come up like, *God couldn't be saying that to me. I'm just making this up.* Be aware of this and trust in faith that what you are hearing is indeed from your Creator. Be bold and speak directly against the author of confusion, Satan, who wants to keep you from this life-giving relationship. Speak boldly against any limitations that you have placed on Jesus. Yell a loud, "No!" to the attacks of fear, shame, doubt, and condemnation. Be confident that God will never speak to you in a way that brings those things.

THE ENEMY WILL TEMPT YOU TO BELIEVE THAT GOD WON'T TALK TO YOU OR THAT HE DOESN'T WANT TO.

I can't wait for your prayers to come alive in your heart. I can't wait for God to give you a tangible reason to worship Him. It will be glorious indeed.

CHAPTER 6

COMMUNITY

HIDING IS THE KRYPTONITE TO HEALING

I was exposed to pornography before I was in middle school," I told my close friend Judy.

Now well into our twenties and thirties, we had similar stories when it came to toxic marriages and divorce. We'd been catching up over lunch. She'd shared with me that her husband's struggle with pornography had been harming their marriage, eventually leading to divorce.

"Wow, really? How were you exposed?" she asked.

"I was lying in my parents' bed, flipping through the channels as my mom slept from all the medicine she'd been having to take." I kept going. "I flipped through the channels, but I couldn't find anything that piqued my interest. For about ten channels it was just black, white, and gray static. Until I hit the seventies, channel seventy-seven to be exact. And there it was, naked men and women having sex and engaging in other things I had no idea about as a ten-year-old. I battled with sneaking around to watching porn in my parents' room, on the family computer, on my smartphone in high school for years."

Her face revealed her shock.

Thinking about her marriage, I reflected, "Pornography is truly an addiction, and it's so sad. Which is no excuse—hear me say that. You didn't deserve your husband's addiction. But I am saying addictions need treatment. And I hope he gets the treatment and freedom that is available."

Judy's husband's struggle with pornography had ravaged their intimacy and trust and had been a big part of what led to their divorce—if not the biggest. In the wake of her divorce, she was left feeling betrayed, disgusted, and heartbroken that the marriage she'd once felt so safe in had become the place where so much hurt and shame was birthed.

After I got home, I realized that I'd never shared my story about porn with anyone. And I felt naked—weird even. I questioned whether we would even be friends anymore. Maybe she thought I was like her ex-husband, and she had been triggered to the point where she'd decide to end our friendship. I was so scared. As I was in mid-panic, a text popped up: "Hey. Thanks for sharing that with me. You didn't have to, and I'm sure it felt weird. But it made me feel seen and less alone. I love our friendship."

She and I are even closer today.

Isn't it so wild how the Enemy of our hearts will attempt to convince us that the very thing that has the power to set us free from hiding will leave us alone and feeling more trapped? The Enemy will use shame to keep us from a life of freedom and healing. *Shame* is a painful feeling of humiliation or distress caused by the consciousness of doing something wrong,[1] or that we perceive as wrong or unacceptable. I believe it's one of his greatest schemes. My team and I have seen it over and over again. When something hard happens to us or creates a negative view of us, we immediately feel regret, sorrow, and the urgency to hide. We stuff our emotions and begin to isolate because of our fear of losing our worthiness, abandonment by our community, and public embarrassment. We can quickly get into a shame bubble and begin to believe that our hiding will lead to healing, and yet it never does. Hiding is the kryptonite to healing. We *need* each other. We need a community of people to look us in the eye and say, "I know everything about you. I know the ins and outs of the depths of your

HIDING IS THE KRYPTONITE TO HEALING.

mistakes and pain. And I love you the same." We need community to be a reflection of Jesus, who whispers those same truths into our hearts.

Author and psychiatrist Curt Thompson, a friend of mine, talks about shame a lot, and he wrote about how it makes us feel at an emotional level in his book *The Soul of Shame*:

> I perceive, beginning at nonconscious levels of awareness, that I do not have what it takes to tolerate what I feel. I am not just sad, angry or lonely. But ultimately these feelings rest on the bedrock that I am alone with what I feel, and no one is coming to my aid. Shame undergirds other affective states because of its relationship to being left. And to be abandoned ultimately is to be in hell. This terror of being alone drives my shame-based behavior and, ironically, takes me to the very place I most fear going—to the hell of absolute isolation.[2]

Shame drives you to the very places of isolation and loneliness we're all so afraid of in the first place. Shame says you don't deserve healing and wholeness. Shame says you don't deserve to be deeply seen and known because if people *really* knew you, they would abandon you. That's a lie from the pit of hell. Let's just call it out for what it is. We can't let shame have the final say in our stories. And we surely cannot let it rob us of community. What has happened to you, and maybe even the regrets that you're carrying, don't get to have victory over your life. The victory has already been won, and now it's time to claim it.

All that sounds great right now. Empowering, even. But it's hard to claim victory when you're face-to-face with the shame of a bad part of your story, isn't it? Have you carried most of it alone? Are there parts of your story that you haven't been honest with other people about? There's no condemnation or blame here, just questions I hope will point you toward the freedom that community can bring.

About 85 percent of the women who go through our women's course on healing say that the thing they loved most was that they were able to go through the course in a safe community. It felt so refreshing and healing to know they were not alone in some of the most painful parts of their stories. Community is important, and in this chapter we'll learn why. We'll even begin discussing practical steps toward creating a healthy community, transitioning toxic people into places that can't affect you, and even how to nurture the community you have well.

SHAME SAYS YOU DON'T DESERVE HEALING AND WHOLENESS.

What *is* community? Community is basically "a group of people living in the same place or having a particular characteristic in common."[3] And even though commonality is one of the bedrocks of friendships, it's even more than that. Community looks like finally finding a safe place and accountability among people who were once strangers and those with whom you've been building relationships for a while, where you eventually become so interwoven in each other's lives that you depend on and show up for one another in all situations.

The people in your community can be your lifeline when everything seems to crush you. They can be the people who stop you from making decisions that can negatively impact your life. They can be the people who make you feel sane, point you to help and restoration, and wipe your tears when your heart can't contain them any longer. They can be the hands and feet of your Savior in your life.

Maybe you're someone who's been negatively affected by community. Maybe a friend lied to you about something, talked about you in a negative way behind your back, or verbally or emotionally manipulated or abused you in some way. You may have even been upset with God for allowing you to experience real pain and tragedy at the hands of someone you'd pulled in close. Author Jenna Carver wrote about this in one of our course modules, saying, "If you're someone who has been hurt by the community you plopped yourself into, it's all too easy to ask the question, 'Why is community even important?'"

I get it. Many of us have experienced that unique pain of being burned by those we once turned to when life felt like the world had burned us. But I'm here to tell you—community is essential, and it has been since the beginning of time. When God made man, do you remember the first thing He noticed about what He had created? That man was lonely. Genesis tells us that God decided that it was "not good for the man to be alone," so He made a companion, someone Adam could do life with (Genesis 2:18).

And that's one of the very first declarations God made: it isn't good for man to be alone. Even before that, we know that God Himself never existed alone—our God's very identity is one of communal existence: He is the Trinity—Father, Son, and Holy Spirit. So when He made us in His own image, that need, that desire— the importance—of being in community was folded into our very character. We see examples of why community is so important throughout the Bible. The writer of Proverbs tells us that community is meant to hold each other accountable and to make each other look more godly than we did when we first entered that community. "As iron sharpens iron, so one person sharpens another" (Proverbs 27:17). Community is where you can find a reflection of God's good intentions: people who know and love you deeply, good and bad, and affirm your belonging.

Jenna Carver went on to make this excellent point in our Hopeful Woman Course material: "Community is also that safe spot where we are able to both grow through our trials and through correction from our friends, but also able to comfortably bring our brokenness, knowing that we will be met with grace and love instead of judgment and exclusion."[4]

> COMMUNITY IS WHERE YOU CAN FIND A REFLECTION OF GOD'S GOOD INTENTIONS: PEOPLE WHO KNOW AND LOVE YOU DEEPLY, GOOD AND BAD, AND AFFIRM YOUR BELONGING.

Jenna is right—this is what community offers to us. While our worth comes from the simple fact that we are created, restored, and loved by our heavenly Father, the tangible presence of the people God has assigned to us here on earth is also a way to keep confirming and reminding us of that, through the love and steadiness they give.

I can remember moments when anxiety and depression reared their ugly heads in my life. And before finding community, I would stuff them down and try to numb or ignore them. I thought, *I'm stronger than those emotions and feelings. They don't matter.* Then, after I became more deeply connected to God in my faith, when those feelings popped up, I would surrender them over to Him. I'd say, "Lord, I can't hold these by myself. I'm not strong enough. I've seen what numbing them and pushing them to the side can do, and I don't want that for myself. I *leak* by losing my temper and lacking focus on the things that matter the most. Help me."

As I grew even more in my faith and understanding of God, I recognized and accepted what Jenna so eloquently wrote: "the desire of being in community was folded into our character."[5] After I'd lost a lot of my community going through divorce, I was alone and felt completely abandoned and forgotten. I began to pray to God and ask Him to give me community that wouldn't hurt or abuse me, that would love me for me, and that I could have for a lifetime. He answered those prayers. And I realized that our Savior is good at community. We saw His undeniable tact when He created man and showed us that he wasn't supposed to be alone by creating Eve shortly afterward. But also when He brought twelve disciples close to walk with Jesus, follow Him, and know Him deeply as He made the ultimate sacrifice for us. It is why we have the historical writings in the New Testament. People recorded what they saw.

Community isn't a replacement for God, but it absolutely works hand-in-hand with our Savior. It's why He created a world where we could coexist with others. But that can only happen when we find the right community. If you have people around you and yet you still don't have what feels like a safe community, you may be living with a toxic community.

IF YOU HAVE PEOPLE AROUND YOU AND YET YOU STILL DON'T HAVE WHAT FEELS LIKE A SAFE COMMUNITY, YOU MAY BE LIVING WITH A TOXIC COMMUNITY.

Talking about toxic community is important because our earthly relationships do impact our heavenly one. The people we have allowed in our lives who have hurt us, betrayed us, and caused wounds we must heal from have a lasting impact on our lives. This is not at all to shame you for decisions you made to allow people into your life. I've chosen people who haven't been the best for my heart. So I feel you, girl! We have to be careful that our hurt from choosing the wrong community doesn't change our ideas about God and how He sees us.

Some people don't or can't stand with you in the darkest valleys of your life. When I went through some of the darkest seasons of church hurt and divorce, I thought certain people would be with me to walk me through. But they were gone, self-preserving and unable to show up and be what I so desperately needed in those seasons. These are probably the types of people who want to be there only in the good times. They aren't willing to walk through your brokenness with you and point you back to hope. This type of relationship could leave you with a feeling of deep abandonment and betrayal. It's important to remember that God is not that way.

It's easy to associate our heavenly Father with our earthly expectations, but that will only give you a God in a box, a God who looks more like the earth He made than the heaven He powerfully dwells in. Deuteronomy 31:6 says, "Be strong and courageous. Do not be afraid or terrified because of them, for the LORD your God goes with you; he will never leave you nor forsake you." Moses was speaking this over all of Israel. This was the last time Moses would be with these people after leading them for forty years. Through slavery, starvation, and struggle, this group of people were tired and weary, but they knew God had something great for them on the other side. And still, when Moses broke the news to them that he would not be going with them, they could've been afraid and upset and heartbroken. But Moses was proclaiming that he knew God was with Israel and would not abandon them on their way to the promised land.

People won't always love you well, but God always will. We will be imperfect, and we will be faulty. We'll forget to show up for each other. We'll say things in haste that we don't mean but that will have lasting effects on those we love. We'll experience brokenness in ourselves and at the hand of others. But one thing remains: God.

He is not faulty, and He'll be there as we pick up our broken hearts and fragile souls. He'll walk with us as we heal and become ready to pursue community again. Because even though some people hurt us, the faithful care of others can be the healing balm that we need.

After my divorce, so many people just vanished out of my life. Some left on their own because they disagreed with me, and others were ripped away when I decided to leave my toxic church right before my divorce. And for many, I had to make the conscious decision to transition them out. I didn't think I would ever have community again. I was afraid to trust anyone new. During that season I got close to God. I let

PEOPLE WON'T ALWAYS LOVE YOU WELL, BUT GOD ALWAYS WILL.

Him fill that void when I had no one else. And then I prayed for new, healthy people. I prayed for God to send me the exact friends I needed to continue my healing journey. And when I think about my close circle of friends now, I'm so glad I mustered up the bravery to trust again. I recognized my own cycles of toxicity that created unhealthy attachments to toxic people. Because of my deep insecurity, I wanted to be liked, so I started people pleasing and becoming whatever people wanted me to be. I would stay in agony in relationships that were bad for me because being alone felt worse. But I healed and found other people who were willing to heal and practice healthy connections. It's been life-changing, truly.

Today I have friends I can reach out to, who will pray fervently for me to experience peace in my greatest anxieties, freedom in the places I feel the most shame, and wholeness in God by pointing me back to Him when I feel empty. I am forever grateful for friends who share in pain, love, and connection with me. Friends who trade my shame for acceptance that no darkness can overshadow.

And I pray that for you. I pray you find your people and hold them close. And I pray, as we put these thoughts of community into action, that you feel equipped and hopeful for the journey ahead. Finding it could look different for you than the people around you. You might find community by joining a small group at your church with folks of a similar age and life stage. Or you might have some Christian friends with whom you've lost touch. Reach out to them and rekindle those friendships that were once so valuable. Notice the solid, mature believers in your neighborhood or your workplace and grab some coffee together. And be open to the possibility that God might surprise you by providing someone you might not expect who will *become* your community. I can't tell you how many women I connected with from a random Instagram giveaway I did who have become prayer warriors for me and soothing voices on the other end of the line.

A girlfriend of mine was befriended by a woman she met online through work, and that little friendship became one of mutual prayer and support, even though they lived in different states! Ask God to provide the community you need. It's a prayer He loves to answer.

LEAVING THE PLACES THAT BROKE YOU

"I've felt betrayed, isolated, and completely forgotten about," Faith said as she told us her story of becoming a widow.

This was in our course on finding hope again after trauma, pain, and hard stories. Faith explained that after her husband passed, all she had was her son. She talked about how grateful she was for him, but also how she felt the burden of being dependent on him and longing for people to see her and know her and tell her she wasn't crazy for being so torn up about it all.

We all fought back tears, with many slipping through and falling down our faces anyway, as we held her tender heart and painful story of feeling forgotten after one of her hardest seasons.

After Faith finished, we poured into her by telling her encouraging words, and then I told her about someone else from our previous course who'd lost her husband, who could not only relate to her story but would see her, know her, and remind her that she wasn't crazy. Her tears stopped falling and her face lit up when we told her that she wasn't alone in this. That there were women who not only knew her story but had walked through a similar time themselves. And guess what? Faith and Jessica, the widow from the previous course, connected and found community together.

We need community. We need to be loved and known all the time, but especially in the darkest parts of our stories. How much more does it mean to you that someone may know the entirety of your story, the good and the real ugly and still say, "I love you and you belong here"? The feeling of being welcomed into friendship while authentically being yourself helps to defeat shame about parts of your story that have been hidden, maybe even from yourself. It brings your heart into a space where trust can grow. And then your heart can be tended to in ways that lead to a life of hope and healing.

Now, the truth is, there are moments in our lives when we also need to eliminate unhealthy behaviors from our hearts. We need healthy boundaries. You may be reading this and have been hurt by a particular community. Maybe friendship has been a place where abuse has entered your story. Sometimes the very people we've brought into our inner circles are the people who have caused the most damage to our hearts and minds.

I don't know what that's looked like for you, but if someone close to you is physically or sexually hurting you, it's not safe to be close with them. If someone continually hurts your self-esteem by using words or emotions to make you feel bad about yourself, that's a toxic relationship. If there's someone who's directly or even indirectly controlling, not allowing you to go places, and making you feel bad for being with other people, that is toxic. If someone is leading you further from God and a life of closeness with Jesus by pressuring you into actions contrary to how God wants us to live, you may not be able to be close to that person. The truth is, you can't heal and find hope in the place that broke you in the first place. Boundaries are necessary to protect us from toxic people—and sometimes so is distance.

> YOU CAN'T HEAL AND FIND HOPE IN THE PLACE THAT BROKE YOU IN THE FIRST PLACE.

Maybe you've found and started to experience wonderful community that has helped you heal, but you still want to understand how to create stability and health that last a lifetime. Maybe you want your relationships to be more than just surface level. And maybe you want to learn how to bring out deeper places of honesty and healing. We didn't take classes in school on how to do friendship and community well. We need tools.

CIRCLES AND BOUNDARIES

Let's talk about friendship circles and boundaries.

Think about your very best friend versus the coworker you just met at work. Your very best friend may be closer to you, know more about you, have more access to you than the coworker. My betrayal trauma counselor, Richard Blankenship, told me, "In order to protect ourselves from toxic emotional harm we have to create boundaries that are strong enough to keep the bad stuff out and permeable enough to let the good stuff in." To create healthy boundaries, we have to figure out where to put relationships in our circles of friendships. Either close, with more access to our hearts and emotions, or a bit further to protect ourselves.

This practice is called setting boundaries. It is just choosing to communicate openly what your personal values are for your mind, heart, and spirit, and being honest about what you will and won't tolerate. It's being able to say, "I don't want to be called this or spoken to like this because it makes me feel like this." And expecting those who love you to uphold them. Boundaries can look different for everyone, but they truly have to be balanced to work. Have your boundaries looked like you holding your hands in a big, fat X where you're denying anyone and everyone from getting close to you so you can be seen and known? Or are your hands completely and carelessly open, where you can become susceptible to harm and abuse?

Could you begin to imagine yourself in a posture that is more optimistic and yet also protective? A stance where you're intentionally keeping the bad stuff out but leaving room for goodness to come into your life? For me that looked like being honest about the relationships I had and assessing whether I should be in the same environments and have the same intimate conversation I'd had before. Could those people tend to my heart during healing seasons like I needed? Or should I keep the conversation light and steer it toward things that didn't impact me greatly? Boundaries are kind to the people you love and who love you. They create a healthy space for your friendships to thrive in healthy ways. When you can set and voice those things that trigger you or upset you, you create a clear guideline for thriving friendships and help people love you well.

One of the hard boundaries I have for my friendships is that we will not call each other demeaning names. Whether it's a joke, or even slightly serious. I believe we are all daughters of a God who has created us to be protected in heart and spirit. When someone calls you and identifies you as something you're not, it's very easy to start living under that label. For instance, "You're fat, girl—you eat so much!" or "You are too much!" While we don't think these types of joking labels affect us, they do. And my friends know I don't want that boundary violated.

Let's talk about the people in your friendship circles. Jesus was particular with His own circles. He was quick to draw a hard line when dangerous people got too close or tried to have a voice in His life contrary to His Father's purpose for Him. Just as it was predicted in Isaiah 53:3–12 that Jesus must suffer, die, and be raised on the third day, when He began to unpack the totality of His mission to the disciples in Matthew 16, Peter rose up in opposition to Jesus. He said, "Heaven forbid, Lord, . . . This will never happen to you!" (Matthew 16:22 NLT). And even though Peter didn't know his words opposed the very purpose Jesus had come to fulfill, Jesus swiftly rebuked him and challenged him (v. 23). Jesus loved Peter dearly, but a boundary had to be set and voiced in order for Peter to stay within His close circle.

Jesus selected twelve people to eat with, travel with, reside with, do ministry with, pray with, challenge, and open up to about His identity and what would be accomplished through Him. He also had circles outside that inner circle that were broader and bigger but less permeable. These included the Pharisees, who were known as judgmental teachers of the Jewish Law. It's not that Jesus completely ignored them, but He didn't let them have the same access to Him as His disciples.

Let's break this down into levels. Jesus' first level was just Him and God, the closest, most intimate relationship. Then level two was Jesus' inner circle, which included Peter, James, and John. Level three, which I like to call the social circle, included the nine other disciples. Level four was Mary, Martha, and other close friends and family. Level five would have included extended social circles and the multitudes, and level six those who were enemies or the lost. When we begin to observe in Scripture the way Jesus interfaced with each of these groups, we can mirror that in our own lives. Rick Thomas says, "Thousands have received Jesus' care, but only a small number of them experienced His direct, undivided, and skilled attention."[6] Jesus understood the importance of drawing a few close to share life with, and He also understood solitude and being alone to connect with His most intimate relationship—with His Father in heaven.

I met with one of my friends in ministry and asked about how she got to a place of close friendship with others as her ministry grew. She'd impacted millions of women around the world through a discipleship model that empowered women to draw closer to Jesus and, from the overflow of that, pour into their communities. I figured she'd have some insight into what it looks like to have a lifestyle change over time and how that affects your friendships. She said something I'll never forget: "Most people think having lots of friends will make you happy, when it's about having a few friends that point you to Jesus, who can bring you real joy." While she had a lot of friends at the beginning of her ministry career, over time many of these friendships no longer brought happiness. So instead, she allowed God to lead her to a few friends who loved her, knew her deeply, and pointed her back to Him.

1. Define Your Circles

The first step to creating healthy community is to notice who is around you and how close you want them to be. What would it look like if you began to imagine all your relationships in circles like the ones pictured below? Would you get more clarity about what to share with whom? Who can hold the deepest and most tender parts of your story, and who just honestly can't? When we allow ourselves to imagine our friends into circles, we begin to respect and honor our hearts and make healthy boundaries that lead to a healthy life.

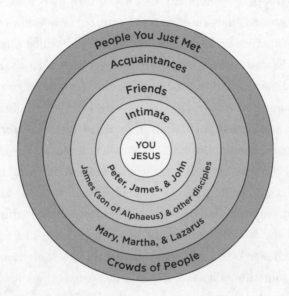

2. Identify Your Needs

Once you've identified who goes into which circle, the second step in creating healthy community is to identify what you need from those friends. These needs will likely vary given your cultural background, the painful or traumatic parts of your story, and the simple fact that we are all uniquely wired to enjoy different things. We all want to be treated in ways that are truly life-giving.

My friend Emma and I were at a coffee shop chatting about how one of her friends had texted her some pretty rude things about her past and used them against her to make a point about a current situation they were working through. While she was in pain and disappointed at how her friend could do something so low, she put on her big-girl pants and decided to confront her about it. She made it very clear that a boundary had been violated and she would appreciate her past weaknesses and situations not being used in disagreements they were trying to process. She made it clear that this was dishonoring to her—to her growth and her heart. I was *so* proud of her. This is such a good example of what it looks like to express your needs!

Paul wrote, "Do not let any unwholesome talk come out of your mouths, but only what is helpful for building others up according to their needs, that it may benefit those who listen" (Ephesians 4:29).

Out of my own insecurities growing up and my desire to be right or perceived as right, I believed I was the expert in everything, and it was very difficult for me to be corrected. My need to make my dad proud after I left the house at sixteen grew into my need to make everyone I encountered proud. I couldn't take criticism. So when it came to how I talked to people I'd get upset, telling them, "This is just the way I talk—deal with it." The honest truth would have been, "I have a deeply rooted insecurity that makes me think more about how perfect I can be than how I can care for others well. I apologize for the way I've treated you. I shouldn't let my unhealth take away from how you should be treated." We all want to be spoken to and loved well, according to our needs. Don't we want friends who are willing to lay down their ideas of what they think a good friend is and pick up what we need? And we don't have to demand these things in a controlling or prideful way. Sometimes we hear, "If I had known that you didn't like that, I wouldn't have done it." Can we believe that we are worthy enough to express our needs about the way we're talked to, supported, and more?

3. Identify What Hurts You

A third aspect of creating healthy community is identifying toxic community. I can remember a time when I was surrounded by toxic community and had no clue until I found healthy community. My old friends wanted to party recklessly and get drunk and high all the time. Many of my friends talked about other people behind their backs. For me, a loving trait is generosity. Many of my friends were not generous. First Corinthians 15:33 says pretty clearly, "Do not be misled: 'Bad company corrupts good character.'" We are deceived when we think we are strong enough to resist what we're around. Our brains respond to patterns and consistencies. When we are exposed to something consistently, our brain becomes conditioned to it. When we change our password to our phones, at first we get it wrong sometimes, then the neurons in our brains begin to catch on and the new password becomes natural to us. So if you're around toxic people, you will more than likely pick up toxic behaviors and traits.

What's also harmful about being in toxic relationships is that our earthly relationships impact our heavenly one. For some of us, the reason our relationship with our heavenly Father is so unhealthy is because our earthly father wasn't there for us when we were children, and we have projected the imperfections of our dads onto our Creator. I have also seen this in religious spaces. If we have a bad relationship with someone in the church, sometimes it dismantles our connection and relationship with God. So we have to be careful. The people we have allowed in our lives who have hurt us, betrayed us, and caused wounds have a lasting impact on us.

We've all made bad decisions about our relationships. Many of us have allowed people to come into our lives who have severely damaged us. Most of the time we didn't know it would turn out that way, and sometimes our past traumas didn't allow us to see the red flags. There's no shame in what you've been through. Instead, I want to shine a light on how we can grow. Let's not allow our hurt to change how we view God and how we believe He sees us. We want to be careful not to develop false perceptions of God because we've chosen the wrong community.

Chelsea, the single mother of a son and one of the women in our first Hopeful Woman Course group, has a beautiful ministry for the fatherless. She helps women process through what it looks like to detach from the false ideas that God is like our earthly fathers who weren't in our lives—that He's abandoned us, He's chosen a different life without us in it, and leaves us to pick up the pieces. I have seen Chelsea totally reframe her view of God, and it's changed the way she talks to God, raises her son, and even helps women who are in the same situation and are looking for ways to get away from toxic relationships and toxic thoughts.

WHAT MAKES A TOXIC RELATIONSHIP?

Here are a few indicators that may point to toxicity.

- **Be wary of people who cut off relationship with you.** Melissa, a woman in our course group, said that her own parents cut her off when she started to pursue counseling and healing and began recognizing their toxic behaviors toward her. She wanted to talk with them about it in a loving way, but they weren't ready to face their own contribution to her pain. So they began ignoring her and not talking to her at all. If there's someone in your life who has completely ended the relationship while you were in a healing season, it could be a potential red flag of toxicity.

- **Notice who discourages you from seeking help and healing.** Often controlling and abusive people don't want the person they're in relationship with to get healing because healthy people have more control over their own lives and begin to set boundaries. They start telling the people who have hurt them ways they need to change to honor them best. I've heard women say that their boyfriends had belittled the idea of counseling or talking to mentors for wisdom. Some even said that they were enough, and the women didn't need anyone else but their boyfriends. This is a conditional, performance-based relationship that's potentially controlling. Look for the people who are willing to walk through your brokenness with you and carry you back to hope. The people who want to see you healthy and whole no matter what that means for the relationship. The people who would rather stay with you and change some of their own toxic behaviors within the relationship to see you flourish.

- **Be cautious about one-sided relationships.** Also beware of one-sided relationships where you're the only one investing. This was something I battled with early on. I felt like I was the only one showing up for my friends, I was the only one listening to their issues without ever being asked about my own, and I was the only one initiating conversations, hangouts, and generosity. In college I was always the one who drove, always the one who bought food, always the one who texted first to hang out and keep the friendship in a good place. Friendship in a healthy community is a balance and exchange of ideas, capacity, and love. Your community should be life-giving and should create a safe place where you can be honest and pour into each other. Are you the only one showing up in the lives of your friends? Are you the only one listening and asking?

Are you the only one giving advice? Are you the only initia-tor in conversations, hangouts, generosity? These are all good questions that can help gauge whether you're in a one-sided relationship.

- **Avoid people who trigger you.** One toxic trait is a bit more obvious: people who frequently trigger you and expose your weaknesses. These people bring up your past mistakes in a critical and hurtful way. I follow a woman on Instagram named Mary whose goal is to lose weight to live a healthier life. She posted a video about a guy she was dating who chose a "healthier" restaurant for one of their dates because he felt like she wouldn't be able to "control herself" in a restaurant with unhealthy foods. When Mary approached him about his choice in dining arrangements and his explanation of why he said those things about her, his response was that if she couldn't control herself from eating habits that made her this size, then she probably still couldn't and would need his help. Can we just say *red flag*? In time, these types of people ulti-mately bring out the worst and most unhealthy version of you. If you are continually triggered by the way they're acting or speaking to you, speak to them about it. If they don't change, it may be time to evaluate their proximity to you. That's not to say these people are bad. They just may have been in your life when you hadn't yet made the decision to be healthier or change behaviors in a specific area. These people may have been crucial to the season you used to be in. But if you're grow-ing into a more hopeful version of yourself, you cannot bring friends along who are not willing to grow with you in the pro-cess. Even worse, they may set you back. You should be asking yourself the question, *Are they growing with me?*

Okay, sis, I know that was a lot. But I want you to be surrounded by the strong, healthy community you need to become the best version of yourself. I hope you will think about who is in your inner circle, what boundaries you need to thrive, and how to identify any toxicity around you. Community is important. As you heal and grow into the woman you were designed to be, make sure there are people around you who are willing to grow as well.

I want to challenge you to pray about this. I remember thinking how weird it was to pray for friends as an adult. It felt lame. But come before your heavenly Father, who knows everything you need, and pray an honest prayer. God could absolutely surprise you as you share your wants and needs out loud with Him. Our heavenly Father is waiting for us, and He can't wait for us to get to heaven. But in the meantime, He wants to see us flourish in joy and peace, love and kindness with the people He's sent into our lives. People who will care for us, reflect Him to us, and cheer us on as we run one of the hardest races we may ever run: the race to be healed and whole.

CHAPTER 7

COUNSELING

LET'S GET PROFESSIONAL

A re you . . . umm, okay?" Jessica asked, jokingly. "I mean, look at all you've been through."

She pointed to the canvas of my life that I'd just verbally processed with her during my first counseling session—all the trauma, divorce, dating Sam, the hard conversation with him after we got married about counseling (more on that later). I'd told her about my mom being sick while I was growing up and my taking care of her. I shared the sexual manipulation, drinking, and drugs at thirteen and fourteen years old. I talked about my eating disorder in college and the toxic marriage and the spiritually abusive church environment.

I responded, "Yeah. I feel great. I mean, it is a lot when you look at it all laid out that way, but I've persevered through it all."

"You did persevere, Toni. And I want you to know that I am so proud of what you did to make it through all that. But what would life look like if you could just . . . live it? Not merely persevere through it. Have you ever imagined a life for yourself where you weren't abused, yelled at, and manipulated? Have you ever called your life peaceful? Do you want that?"

Tears welled up in my eyes. I hadn't thought about that. I didn't know it was possible. Thoughts began to race through my head as tears dropped from my eyes.

"I mean, could you be in a loving relationship in which someone didn't curse you out? Or yell at you? Is that even love? Is there a life that doesn't require me to have to claw my way through it all the time? I do want that. I want peace—I do."

She handed me a tissue to wipe my tears and blow my now leaking nose. I realized that in that moment, I was officially starting the journey to healing and wholeness through professional care. And, Jessica, my first counselor, was going to be my guide.

Counseling changed my life, and we're going to talk through it, dispel some myths, and lean into what the Bible says about it. You may be hesitant about counseling. Maybe you have heard that it's only for "crazy people" or people with serious mental health issues. I know in African American culture, seeking help from a therapist has often been framed as a negative thing. My parents still kind of cringe when I talk to them about counseling because in the past it was viewed as something that you didn't do, and surely didn't talk about. What's your history with counseling? You may have started a counseling journey and just didn't enjoy your counselor and quit. You may have started a counseling journey and gotten to the part where you had to go back and relive parts of your story that just sucked and scared you. Or maybe you're in counseling right now and it's going great.

Wherever you are in this journey, I want to encourage you to think through this chapter with intentionality. This part of the road map God has given us can help us through the messy parts of our stories. That is meaningful and, yes, hard as heck. But so worth it. It's not an "Okay, I did some counseling sessions; I should be good to go" kind of thing. It's leaning in and pressing into the crushed parts of our lives. It's the maintenance of our minds and hearts, and it's a marathon—a forever thing.

My personal counseling journey hasn't ended. I started with Jessica, working on identifying the trauma and pain from my childhood. In our weekly sessions, for two years, we addressed chronic insecurity, severe anxiety, depression, and suicidal ideation. We talked through how I would prefer agony over being alone and how to change my mindset of being alone versus just feeling lonely. And that I was never alone. We did rounds of EMDR, or eye desensitization and reprocessing therapy. (Sis, that was a hard one.) It is a form of psychotherapy that helps you heal from the symptoms and emotional distress that come with traumatic memories.

Then I needed Carl, my second counselor. He's a betrayal and sexual trauma therapist whose practice also offered a sixteen-week trauma group course. I needed to go through it to heal from past relationships that were sexually manipulative and filled with pornography and betrayal. But it doesn't stop there! My husband, Sam, and I have gone to marriage counseling intensives and have a marriage counselor for upkeep in our relationship. I am also in a small group now that focuses on mental health and defeating shame through community and inviting God into our hearts together. And last, I have a counselor named Rachel who helps me manage my own mental and emotional upkeep, and I will probably have her for as long as she'll keep me.

I know what you're thinking: *Woo, Toni, that is a lot, girl.*

We must take our mental and emotional health seriously. We want to do our best to invest in it, learn and do our research, and, most importantly, show up as our full selves. When you're in need of advice in any of these areas, sure, talking to a friend can be extremely helpful. Community is extremely important, as we learned earlier. But just as doctors study the human body to understand its medical needs, counselors have studied the human mind and how it interfaces with our mental and emotional challenges.

WE MUST TAKE OUR MENTAL AND EMOTIONAL HEALTH SERIOUSLY.

There are some things your bae cannot fix, your bestie cannot fix, because they just don't know how to. The people in your close circles can listen and validate your feelings and past hurt. They can even help you navigate your feelings and walk with you to the other side of healing and hope. I know that building close circles is a difficult thing and you may not even have those in your life yet. I believe it's coming for you as you ask God to provide the community you need. And when you do have those circles built, know that even as amazing as they will be, those people can't diagnose you or connect your present suffering with your past wounds.

Counselors have studied the human mind, and not only do they understand how our neurons wire together to create the thoughts and behaviors that govern our mindset, but they also have access to proven solutions that can help us process and heal in healthy ways. There's growth and healing available for you. There's a better version of yourself waiting on the other side of your decision to be brave enough to go to counseling.

A counselor's goal is to help make you the best version of yourself, but it's not only for you; it's also for the people you influence. And *you* bring *you* with *you*—everywhere. We've discussed that who you are, in your unhealth, leaks onto other people. Isn't it selfish to stay in that place, knowing that you are negatively affecting the people you say you love? You may leak onto your children by yelling and punishing them too harshly when you feel embarrassed or ashamed by something they've done. You may come home and dump all your emotional baggage from work on your spouse or significant other by blaming them. You may even lose your temper at work because of the pressures and pains you feel at home.

Our emotions, good or bad, don't choose specific relationships to affect. When we are unhealthy women, we're also unhealthy wives, mothers, daughters, and friends. The unhealthy parts of us are not isolated to one area. They leak on all of them. So, why counseling? We want to be whole women who create whole communities, whole relationships, and, for moms or future moms, a legacy of emotional health for our children. God has a plan and a purpose for each of us, and whether you're in leadership on stages, on your campus, or even in your household, you have a responsibility to be the healthiest version of you.

I hope you don't feel like I'm pointing a finger at you or scolding you. My urgency comes from a place of familiarity. I remember when I leaked on my daughter, husband, and everyone else close to me. I still hold a bit of regret tucked in my heart today. I'd just come out of my divorce, started to rebuild my life, got into an apartment with my daughter, finally got a job, and then started dating. I remember how hard parenting was. I yelled more times than I offered up patience and grace. I was always on edge.

I remember a moment when Dylan was in children's church and had a meltdown. Because of my need to be the best in the room, her actions completely triggered me and made me feel so much shame. I took that out on her by screaming and yelling about her behavior instead of consoling her and walking her through it. I even kept her from going to her best friend's birthday party as a punishment—something she remembers to this day. I chose my insecurities over gentleness and patience with my daughter. I was leaking on her.

In that season, I'd completely excommunicated myself from all my friends. Everyone felt unsafe to me because I'd been hurt by so many people I trusted. I felt I couldn't trust anyone. So I hid in an isolated place of shame, fear, and anxiety. I couldn't perform at my new job well. I wouldn't answer phone calls or emails from the few people who genuinely cared, because depression had settled in, and everything became numb. There were so many moments when I just didn't feel like getting out of bed.

My husband, Sam, who was my boyfriend at the time, got the worst of me. We'd have a very simple conflict, like him telling me something I said bothered him, and I would completely melt down.

I didn't want to do anything wrong with him because I didn't want him to leave me, or, in my mind, abandon me. I couldn't admit that I had done something wrong—even the smallest thing. I couldn't apologize because I just didn't want to be at fault. Mistakes in my past had meant I wasn't good enough. Mistakes meant I was going to be yelled at or, worse, left. I would be triggered by simple things like his going to work, thinking he was abandoning me. I would call and text over and over again and smother him with my insecurities. I'd fish around for reasons to start a fight so all his attention would be on me. I was so used to chaos that peace felt foreign. I was being crushed under the weight of unhealth without professional help. But worse, all my relationships were being crushed as well.

I needed help or I would damage my daughter even more than the impact of divorce. I needed a space to process my pain or I would stay isolated and depressed without anyone to look me in the eye and say, "I know your pain and I know your deepest mistakes, and I still love you the same." I needed counseling or I would lose the one man who wanted to love my daughter and me unconditionally.

So, after we were married, one day Sam looked me in the eyes and said, "I think you need to go to counseling or we're going to lose this."

It was the day I broke free from shame, isolation, and the wallowing pit of emotional and mental toxicity, but it was tough to admit. We were sitting in the half-empty room that would soon be our office. It was so difficult to respond; tears just came down.

"But I don't want to go," I finally choked out. I'd remembered how taboo it was to go to counseling. How my parents had frowned upon it so much. How it was for "crazy" people. Was I a crazy person?

Sam responded, "I know, but you need to. We can't keep going like this. We're going to lose this."

He was right. And I didn't want to lose my new marriage. That was the day I vowed I would pursue the healthiest, most whole version of myself. And I want that for you, sister. More than anything.

OVERCOMING THE MYTHS

Myth 1: Counseling Means a Lack of Faith

One common myth is that going to counseling means you lack faith in God. Lies and deception! This idea couldn't be further from the truth. Many of us grew up in churches that said if you went to see someone for your mental and emotional health it meant that you didn't think God was a Healer. It meant that you'd allowed the Enemy to take over your heart and mind. For far too long Christians have been afraid to talk about the common struggles of mental and emotional health in fear that they would be told to just suck it up or pray about it.

Well, first, counselors don't heal you, God does. A counselor is a resource for your healing, but God is and should always be your ultimate Source. I once read an article that talked about the idea that therapy doesn't mean that there's a lack of faith. One of the analogies I loved was thinking about our minds and hearts like a broken limb. Imagine this: you have a broken limb, you go to the doctor, and they patch you right on up. Maybe with a brace or a cast. Well, you will likely leave the doctor's office with that same broken limb, and over time your body will heal itself because that's the way God has miraculously made us. That doctor did not heal you; God's design did.[1] But what the doctor did do was provide you with guardrails and instructions to help activate the healing power of God.

That's what counselors do for us. They provide guardrails down a path to verbally processing our thoughts, emotions, and experiences. Counselors give us instructions and sometimes even strategies to help us get on the other side of trauma. Proverbs 12:15 says, "A stubborn fool considers his own way the right one, but a person who listens to advice is wise" (GW). I want to encourage you to find a counselor who understands the role they play alongside God. It would be wise to get a licensed Christian counselor who is submitted to God and unashamed to bring Him into your counseling sessions.

Myth 2: Counseling Works over a Specific Time Frame

A second myth insists that our healing should be quick. As I mentioned, I've never seen a linear healing journey, and I've surely never seen one that's fast. I've also never seen a healing journey that's looked like someone else's. Just as our stories and pain are unique to what we've experienced, so is the way we heal and process. It can depend on how often your counseling sessions happen, how willing you are to open up with your counselor, and how committed you are to doing the work outside of counseling.

We shouldn't fall into the healing comparison trap. We can easily start to think things like, *Well, my friend went to counseling for six months and she's much better. Why aren't I?* Or, *It's been four months. Why am I not getting better?* When I had thoughts like those, my counselor told me, "Toni, you've spent twenty-five years of your life in toxic and abusive environments. You have been being wired for more than two decades to think that your worth is contingent on your performance professionally or sexually. A few months of seeing me isn't going to dismantle the thoughts that have become bad habits in the neural network of your mind. We must destroy those thoughts with care, and rebuild them, one strategy, one thought, and one prayer at a time. That will take time." And boy, was she right. My friend, psychiatrist Curt Thompson, explains it like this:

Transformation requires a collaborative interaction, with one person emphatically listening and responding to the other so that the speaker has the experience, perhaps for the first time, of "feeling felt" by another. The interpersonal interaction exposes these functions of the mind and facilitates the integration of various layers of neural structures and brain systems, which in turn creates new neural networks.[2]

When you sit with someone like a counselor who sees and hears your pain, you feel that much more felt and known. And when we feel more known, our guards come down and we can allow hope to settle in. When you do that over time, you heal over time. And in the months and years to come, you'll be able to look back like me and say, "Wow, what a journey. But it was so worth it."

God is on your side in this healing journey. God wants this particular part of your being to be healed—your mind. Ephesians 4:23–24 says, "Let the Spirit renew your thoughts and attitudes. Put on your new nature, created to be like God—truly righteous and holy" (NLT). Your righteousness and holiness don't just come from a good heart and a good soul, although those things matter a lot to God. They also come from having a renewed mind and renewed ways of thinking and being in the world. Renewing your mind means creating new and healthy thinking patterns about yourself and others. It's about conditioning your mind to be positive, aware of toxicity, and able to identify when something is not healthy for you.

GOD IS ON YOUR SIDE IN THIS HEALING JOURNEY.

Curt Thompson makes an important point about this:

God never connects with us simply to make us feel safe or loved. His transformation always includes a command (a word against which our tendency is to rail) to follow him to the remaining places within ourselves and the world where darkness, cruelty, injustice, and rebellion persist. He invites us to go into deeper places within ourselves and within the world, both ventures requiring a greater degree of faith, hope and love.[3]

Curt is saying here that God has more for you. He not only wants us to *feel* safe and loved but He also wants us to act like it. He wants us to continue to pursue an even more beautiful and healed life than we can imagine. And that happens by going deeper with Him.

God wants you to go deeper, sis. He wants you to bravely go into those dark, broken places that have left you in despair and grab hope and light out of them. When we go into deeper places within ourselves, we can go deeper into our relationships, communities, and our world. Let's explore some practical steps on how to find a counselor and how to show up to counseling prepared and ready to do the work. If you're not already in counseling, there are so many reasons I hope you consider it. And if you are doing the work with a counselor, I want to validate and commend you for doing a work of renewal and restoration. Mental and emotional freedom is on the other side of your yes to counseling—I promise. I've taken the step myself, and I've seen countless lives restored because of it. Let's get to work.

TOOLS AND DEEP BREATHS

I want to tell you about a slightly funny but pivotal moment in my life. I was living it up in college in Texas as a freshman at Sam Houston State. I mean, I was partying like crazy, visiting different schools (and the guys at those different schools, if you know what I mean). I was dancing all over the parties and sweating so hard my outfit and hair were as drenched as if I'd jumped into a pool. I was barely ever in my dorm, and when I was, I was scarfing down ramen noodles, pepperoni Hot Pockets, and wine coolers. I took full advantage of the cafeteria buffet meals, and all that added up to the infamous "freshman fifteen" weight gain. My clothes stopped fitting, I started feeling sluggish, and my friends had the wide-eyed, "Toni, is that you?" look on their faces when they saw me.

Being the Enneagram three achiever I am, I hit the gym. Every morning, I would do a workout program called Beachbody P90X, an intense, ninety-minute-a-day, three-month program with weights and cardio. Working out this hard, I just knew that I would be fit and way hotter in no time. I was wrong. So very wrong. After working out each day I would go to the cafeteria buffet and load up on the fresh waffles, devour more Hot Pockets for lunch and dinner, and drink and party all night. When a friend told me, "Abs are made in the kitchen," I ignored it and thought, *Surely I don't have to sacrifice food for a great body*. Wrong again.

Working out intensely every morning wasn't the issue. I was showing up at the gym. But the issue was what I was willing to give up to get the body I wanted. And that's how we can approach counseling.

Some of us think talking to our friends and family about our healing journey is enough. Others find the right counselor, show up to the sessions, pay the money, and think they're good to go. We can refuse to create boundaries or not go into spaces that have harmed us before, and ruin our healing progress. We can be genuinely focused on our healing but forget the intricate sacrifices and focus it takes to heal well. Yes, technically we're "working out." But we haven't done the "kitchen" work. What I'm saying is that it takes more than just dwelling in healing spaces; it takes *doing* in healing spaces. Putting in the work to dig deep into our stories, be vulnerable, set the boundaries, transition our community, and face the reality that this is hard work.

I want to talk about the *how* behind counseling. We've talked about *what* it is and even how important it is. But now let's talk about our part. How do we show up? How do we heal well? And most importantly, how do we find the counseling we need with little to no resources?

1. Reject Shame

Don't be ashamed. I say this often, but it's something I think we must revisit over and over again. Often shame will keep us from pursuing counseling. Shame can tell us that we don't deserve to be healed. Shame will whisper that we'll always be a victim, knowing that Jesus, our victor, has already won it all. Now, this isn't to say that you won't feel emotions of shame; we all do. Shame rears its ugly head in some of our most dreadful situations and even in some of our happiest moments. It tells us we will only know darkness— while we're down, and even when we're clawing our way to light. This nasty scheme of the Enemy prevents us from fully engaging in counseling. But, sis, hear my words: your healing is an investment in yourself and one of the bravest things you'll ever do. Don't let the Enemy win this one. Go do the work.

2. Find a Counselor

Finding a counselor can be overwhelming, but trust me when I say it's worth it. If you're in college, try the counseling center on campus. If there isn't one, try your college doctor, who can refer you to one in your insurance network. If you aren't in college, start with your doctor. There are also many counselor search engines online such as GoodTherapy and BetterHelp. Or check with your employer. There may be an employee assistance program that will help financially. If finances are an issue, try your local church; as you get connected, they may be able to start you off with a few sessions with someone on staff, but I highly recommend a licensed professional for long-term healing. There are also nonprofits such as the Lighthouse Network that have free hotlines that set up sessions at low costs for those battling with their mental health. Last, the US Department of Health and Human Services can help with finding low-cost or free counseling.

3. Be Selective in Choosing a Counselor

This is a big one! Know that all counselors aren't the same. I know, bummer. Counselors are human. They have different personalities and different areas of focus. If you try a counselor for a few visits who you don't love, it's totally okay to look for another one you may connect with better. I've had friends rave about their counselors and tell me I should give them a try. But they weren't a good fit for me. A counselor may be a good fit for a friend but not for you, and that's totally okay. Another thing to consider is that if you find yourself consistently leaving your sessions feeling worse, you may want to think about getting a new counselor. There will be moments when you feel drained or triggered, but if progressively and over time you're feeling worse than when you started, you should consider changing counselors.

What you should feel from your counselor is safety and reassurance first. Have they ensured confidentiality and worked toward building trust with you? You should also feel that they're equipped to handle the weight of what you're carrying. What certifications, experience, and wisdom do they have to offer? After every session, you should feel like you were able to verbally process your thoughts and emotions. You should leave with the belief that you were seen and heard. And while the tension you're battling through may not be resolved after a one-hour session with your counselor, you should feel a sense of closure on the conversation after that specific session.

4. Expect the Healing Process to Be Uncomfortable

Here's a hard truth: it may get worse first. Because you will be unpacking the brokenness in your life, things will be revealed that have hurt you and caused deep pain. There will be moments when you ask yourself, *Why am I putting myself through this?* And that's valid. This is the healing process. It's the unraveling and identifying of pain, in order to treat it and get to healed places. And, friend, to get to healed places you have to know the pain in your story.

Remember when I was curled up at the bottom of that staircase, pleading for God to take the pain away? That was after I'd started counseling, not before. I'd allowed myself to identify and feel the pain, and it hurt. But you know what? God met me there when I was curled up. But also He met me at my counseling sessions, and in my car driving away after hearing something from my counselor that crushed me to accept. God was there with me, and He'll be there with you as well. This is why I'm so glad you're diving into this book.

Your knowledge that healing is painful will help you cope with that pain when it comes. Maybe for you the word *pain* itself is cringeworthy. But this is how your grit grows. This is how you get stronger and braver: by working out your emotional and mental muscles. By remembering and identifying the pain, then giving yourself the tools to overcome it both now and later.

5. Expect the Healing Journey to Take Time

Remember—your counseling journey isn't a sprint; it's a marathon. One of the things I tell the women in our healing course is to pace themselves. Not because I don't think they're strong enough or brave enough to handle it all, but because I've had to pace myself. My counselor has had to slow me down in moments when I wanted to tackle my way through healing. Who would you be racing against? Your enemies? Your abuser? No. The people who hurt you don't get any more power over you. Your healing is yours. Your hope is yours. And you're not proving to anyone that you can somehow be the fastest to heal from the pain they caused you.

As my friend Cassandra Speer says, "This is hard and holy work that you're doing, friend." The hard rarely goes fast, and the holiest of holies, our Savior, Jesus, doesn't even operate on our timetable. Healing doesn't happen overnight. You won't go to a few counseling sessions and come away completely healed. When you sign up for counseling, you're signing up to walk, not run, down a path that intentionally looks at the depths of your painful experiences and helps you gracefully claw your way out of them. I know, that's super intense. But you were made to be whole from the inside out. God made you to be whole, even in the midst of the devastating sin that surrounds us.

6. Stay Open and Expect God to Meet You

Your heart's posture is important. When you begin counseling, dig deep and do the work. If you go into counseling close-minded, doubtful, and unengaged, that's what you'll receive in return. I want to introduce a term to you: *hope-postured*. Being hope-postured means that you're activating your belief that God has good for you on the other side. It means that even when it absolutely hurts, when it feels impossible, a part of you knows hope is coming. It'll be easier at times to have a posture of hope. It may even feel effortless. Then there will be times when it's easy to feel hopeless, and that's when you get to remember that there's power in your posture. There's power in the way you think and feel about your healing journey.

7. Do the Work

You play a major part in your counseling journey. While your counselor has a professional obligation to fulfill his or her role, you have a part to play in contributing to your healing as well. So when your counselor asks you to do homework, to reflect or journal something, or even pray about something, *do it*. While this isn't a race, doing your homework outside of counseling can help you stay on track at a steady pace of healing.

8. Embrace Vulnerability

Being vulnerable with your counselor is something practical you can do to make counseling more effective. It doesn't have to be during your very first session, but the quicker you can open up about the depths of your story, the quicker your counselor can help you heal. Like me, you may have some hard parts of your story—some you haven't even had the strength to admit honestly to yourself. But hiding leads to shame, and if we are going to break free from shame, we have to remember that our counselor's office is a safe place and one of the places we can be open and honest in confidence.

9. Welcome Support from Your Community

Accountability outside of your counselor is important as well. This goes back to having community around you to help hold you up. It's so important to have one or two close friends who know about the counseling part of your healing journey. Friends could play a part by checking in on you, holding your hand when things get tough and you need a moment of reassurance, and covering you in prayer as you tackle hard things. Think about someone you're willing to be completely open and honest with, someone you trust and can be safe with, who has the capacity to pour into you when you have nothing else left to give.

10. Be Patient in Hope

After almost two years of counseling, I'd hit a wall. I'd processed through my childhood story, tackled insecurity head-on, looked at my anxiety and how it was causing troubles with my sleeping, and gone through sleep training and meditation strategies, and I just kept getting triggered by things in my marriage, parenting, and career. I remember getting on my knees and asking God to lead me and show me what else to do. If I'm honest, I felt defeated. I'd done the work of counseling; I'd sat in the counselor's office every week for two years. And at that point I wasn't aware that there was anything else that could be done. But here's what got me through the week of waiting until my next counseling session. David, the writer of the Psalms, expressed a moment of deep sorrow and doubt:

> Have mercy on me, LORD, for I am faint;
> heal me, LORD, for my bones are in agony.
> My soul is in deep anguish.
> How long, LORD, how long?
> Turn, LORD, and deliver me;
> save me because of your unfailing love.
> Among the dead no one proclaims your name.
> Who praises you from the grave?
> I am worn out from my groaning.
> All night long I flood my bed with weeping
> and drench my couch with tears.
>
> (PSALM 6:2–6)

At first glance, these are pretty dark words. But as a believer who grew up in cultures that say "counseling" and "Christ" don't fit together, and as someone who has thought that mental health and emotions don't align with my faith, this was reassuring. Here was

King David of Israel being honest about where he was. I've had tears that drenched my couch and I've wept in my bed too. So to know that someone with great faith after God's heart felt the same helped me not feel so alone.

What Worked for Me

These words from Psalms gave me the strength to walk into my counselor's office and boldly ask her if there was something else we could do to dig even deeper.

And there it was: EMDR.

Eye movement desensitization and reprocessing therapy. A mouthful, right? But it's a form of psychotherapy that has changed my life and reconciled some of the most horrific moments of my past. And this is just one form of therapy; there are many others that may suit your needs in beautiful ways, from story therapy to therapy that helps manage your sensory system to other forms that can best deal with your particular needs.

Jessica, my counselor, explained it to me this way. Imagine your life is a bookshelf, and your story is made up of the books moving left to right. When trauma is introduced in your life, it's almost as if a book is just slightly pulled out. Causing your thoughts, feelings, communication—everything to process from left to right, but with that traumatic event in the way. Imagine how you would react to failure, an ended relationship, being let go from that job *if* that book wasn't slightly pulled out. Well, EMDR takes the most traumatic moments of your past and helps your brain reconcile them—not to forget them, but to heal from them in a way that just pushes the book back in. You allow your thoughts, emotions, and communication a clear pathway to work through.

Now, maybe you haven't had any trauma in your life, but it's possible you don't know you did, like me. Maybe you've always wondered what makes you react the way you react and feel the way you feel. Would you do your heart a favor and talk with your counselor about EMDR? It may be an effective treatment for you that could change the way the rest of your life could look.

I know that was a lot. Can we deep breathe together? Breathe in for four seconds, hold it for four seconds, and exhale for six seconds. Again. And one more time.

Let's break this down into practical counseling journey steps:

1. If you're not already in counseling, start doing your research.
2. If you just started counseling, do your homework.
3. If you've been going to counseling for a while, share about it with an accountability partner.

Wherever you are on your counseling journey, I want you to know that I am so proud of you and your pursuit of healing and wholeness. I can't wait to see your weeping turn to dancing and your tears be wiped away by our heavenly Father in the days to come. You've got this!

CHAPTER 8

GRATITUDE

SOMETIMES IT'S OKAY
TO REMEMBER

When I was in college, working as a camp facilitator on the weekends, my parents let me use the family car by myself for the first time. I couldn't wait to wake up and drive myself to work on Saturday mornings! That was a big deal for me. I'd lost my parents' trust in high school after I'd snuck out of the house multiple times and *stole* my parents' car to visit an older guy who was manipulating me. I can still remember my mom's anger the night they caught me coming home from a joy ride in their car. But they chose to forgive me, and trust between us had been rebuilt. This was my chance to prove myself, and I was going to do everything I could to keep that trust. Or so I thought.

When my parents dropped the car off for me, they said two things. "Don't be textin' and drivin' and don't be speedin'."

"I won't!" I said. "You guys don't even worry about me."

I remember lying in my small dorm bed, texting all my friends. I was so excited that I had a car to myself, could get around campus and my college city as I pleased, and was even going to get up in the morning and drive myself to work.

Less than twenty-four hours later, I totaled the car.

That's right, sis. I was speeding and texting and driving, of course, at the tender age of seventeen. That's right, seventeen. I'd graduated from high school on a dual credit program at sixteen and there I was, seventeen and immature. Driving recklessly with no consequences in mind. When I looked up and saw the stop sign at the camp entrance, I hit the brakes in the slippery rain, skidded all over the road, and hit a tree so hard the engine came through the car. My arms were bruised from the airbag explosion. I was in shock and so afraid that I was shaking and crying. The gate attendant opened my door and pulled me out of the car. He asked if I was okay, and all I could say between fear and checking to see if anything was bleeding or broken was, "I need to call my parents."

An hour later, my parents rolled in. I expected rage from my dad. But when he got out of the car, I saw fear in his eyes for the first time in my life. He didn't say a word. There was just silence and heavy breathing. My mom rushed over to me, looking for anything broken, and hugged me.

Can I be honest, though? A year later my parents finally bought me a car of my own, and while driving back to my college apartment one night I was texting and driving *again*, after having had a few drinks, and skidded on the highway into a ditch. I got out of my car to walk around, check the damage, and pull the grass from my tires. A man had pulled over and was standing at the top of the ditch.

The helpful stranger called out, "Hey, ma'am! I saw what just happened. Wow, I'm glad you're okay. Do you need help?"

I politely waved and said, "No thank you! Looks like everything is fine."

This time there was no damage to my car. I slowly drove out of the ditch, back onto the road toward my apartment. I was spooked for sure, but I'd shaken it off, turned my music up loud, and made it home like nothing had even happened.

Not even four years later—you guessed it—I was driving with a friend, this time with wine glasses in our hands and the music blasting loud. The road was wet, and as I was speeding and coming around a loop on the highway, my tires skidded. We completely spun around, banged my car on a concrete barrier, and were facing on-coming traffic. My friend was petrified. I turned the car off, restarted it, and put it in reverse to try to get it to turn around the correct way on the highway. It took a few tries, but finally we were facing the right way and began to drive off. Not even three seconds later cars flooded in behind us. It was truly a miracle. But again, I shook it off and dropped my friend home in my now smashed-in red hatchback Toyota Yaris, acting like nothing had happened. I remember turning the music on and belting out songs on the way to her house. There was a moment when I looked over and caught my friend thanking God that we made it out alive. She didn't say a word for the rest of the car ride.

Three times, three different points in my life. You may be thinking, *Toni, why were you so reckless? Why didn't you learn from the first time and drive more cautiously? Or even the second time?* For most people, one car accident would've traumatized them so badly they might not have wanted to ever drive again, or at the very least they would have started driving more carefully. I think because I'd experienced so much tragedy in my childhood, so many near-death experiences and emergency room visits with my mom, and I'd been sexually manipulated, that I'd become numb to it. And I didn't have much to live for. In college all I knew was being used during sex with random guys, being disconnected from my family to protect my heart, and partying with drugs and alcohol to continue the numbing. I only knew chaos. It was like living in a haze with no care in the world. And it wasn't just car accidents. This was the way my whole life functioned. I'd get into an abusive relationship, leave, and then go right back to it. I'd become numb to the pain and connected to trauma in an unhealthy tethering to a life of darkness and deep sorrow.

Have you ever been there? So numb to trauma and pain that even the hard things don't faze you? Have you grown accustomed to being yelled at? Called names? Are you used to violent outbursts? Have you ever woken up and asked yourself why you made those decisions last night? Maybe you feel ashamed and embarrassed for the moment, but still find yourself in the same situations, with the person who hurt you, time and time again. Perhaps you've run back to the same situation because agony there felt better than loneliness. Or maybe the pain and trauma you're experiencing now has crushed you in such a devastating way that you don't have the strength to fight back, to fight for better, to get up and get out. So instead, you fold under the weightiness of staying in pain rather than fighting for hope. Well, I see you, and I know the depths of strength it takes to claw your way out of the deep valleys.

When I transitioned out of my toxic marriage and abusive church and started my healing journey, it was painful. It wasn't the beautiful, happy ending we see in the movies. It wasn't like that moment you get rescued out of your situation and, *boom*, everything is filled with light. No more darkness invades your life. Everything is made new in an instant. That's not how healing was for me. It wasn't linear, and it wasn't pretty. I thought there would be a flip of some switch and my life would be easier. After all, I was the one who mustered up the bravery to leave the toxic environments I'd been stuck in. But it wasn't that easy. After two years outside of toxic environments and doing the hard work of counseling and growth, I was tired of the panic attacks, the PTSD (post-traumatic stress disorder), and the anxiety keeping me from sleeping. I was in a new, beautiful marriage, but I just couldn't get out of the trauma of my past. I didn't want to live anymore. If healing hurt this bad, why in the world would I want to continue this? Trauma hurts, abuse hurts, and now healing hurts.

I remember when my suicidal thoughts turned to suicidal ideation. I went from just thinking about taking my life, to ideas about how to actually do it. At first, I just thought, *What would it be like if I just wasn't here on this earth anymore? Would it be easier?* And now I was thinking about ways to end my life. I held a Nyquil bottle while standing in my kitchen and thought about drinking all of it so I could go to sleep and never wake up again. I didn't know if it would kill me or not, but part of me hoped it would.

Healing just hurt too much. It was too hard. But when I stood there barefoot, slouched over the kitchen sink, I closed my eyes and I remembered. I remembered my dad's face when I wrecked my car. Full of fear and silence, his body breathing heavily. He'd later told me that he didn't have any words because when he saw the car, he was just so grateful that I was alive that he couldn't speak. I remembered my friend silently whispering a thank you to God for sparing us during that wine-fueled car accident. I remembered what it was like to almost die but somehow be rescued out of it. And for the first time I realized that all the while, God was watching over me. He was sparing my life. He was holding me and protecting me from the dangerous situations I'd put myself in.

And in that moment, something new washed over me: *gratitude*. Somehow, in that moment, I was just so grateful to be alive.

As I set down the Nyquil bottle I'd been clutching, with tears streaming down my face, my husband Sam came rushing into the kitchen. He heard my wild cries, and he knew the pain I'd been suffering from. His pounding footsteps on our second-floor apartment tile stopped, and he locked eyes with me. He saw the tears and noted my posture. He spotted the Nyquil bottle before I'd set it down and asked what was going on. I told him I didn't want to live anymore, and I thought I needed some help. He phoned a friend who was a counselor, and once again my life was spared. I remember being in our bedroom with his friend on speakerphone. He said he understood how difficult my journey had been and that everything would be okay. He asked me how counseling was going and how my daughter Dylan was. He was reminding me of the good things.

I want you to lean into this moment with me. I'd engaged in counseling during these years of healing, which provided the resources I needed to make it through some of the darkest seasons of my life. But it was gratitude that gave me deep hope to choose to live again. Gratitude saved my life. Gradually I began to remember that God saw me in every single season of my life, from bad choices to toxic relationships to completely forgetting about Him, and He hadn't left me. I became so grateful that He stuck around, kept choosing me, and was always reaching for me, wanting me to reach back. Gratitude filled my heart.

In our women's course on hope and healing, we explain gratitude to participants this way:

> Gratitude is how we take back our thoughts from the Enemy's hands. First, gratitude exists as a response to the realization that life is a gift, and one that we receive every day, so we peel our eyes open and breathe again. Then it becomes a fruit or outcome of putting all our trust in Jesus and believing in His promises despite our present circumstances. But also, it is a warrior pose, an attack stance. When the very real feelings of fear, anxiety, worry, depression, and loneliness start to creep in, gratitude is our weapon.[1]

I almost imagine gratitude like that whack-a-mole game. Every time a dark thought pops up, *WHAM*—I'm shutting it down with a handful of gratitude. Every time I find myself complaining or irritated, *WHAM*—I'm slamming it down with gratitude.

And here's the deal: we aren't the first to recognize that gratitude is a weapon that can carry us to renewed hope and a life of true wholeness. Make no mistake, the Enemy doesn't want us living in hope. He never has. So just like God's beloved children who came before us, we have to bravely fight using the very tools that God has given us. One of them is gratitude.

Countless instances in the Bible demonstrate how powerful gratitude is and how God responds to it. Daniel had extremely strong faith and expressed his gratitude to God no matter what happened. Daniel was told that anyone who worshipped any God other than the royal master Darius the Mede would be thrown into a lion's den (aka *murdered*). Daniel continued to pray daily to the God of Israel. And while the king, who loved Daniel, was distressed about his decision, he still had to cast him to the pit. As soon as morning came, the king rushed to the pit and cried out asking if God had saved his friend Daniel. Daniel replied from the pit that the God of Israel, his God, had sent an angel to close the jaws of the lions and spared his life.

But before Daniel went into the pit, Scripture says, "Now when Daniel learned that the decree had been published, he went home to his upstairs room where the windows opened toward Jerusalem. Three times a day he got down on his knees and prayed, giving thanks to his God, just as he had done before" (Daniel 6:10). Daniel chose to give thanks to God and worship Him, even in the face of death. God heard his prayers. God recognized Daniel's great faith and his belief that God was good. And even if Daniel was devoured in a pit of lions, he was going to give God thanks.

Another story of gratitude is found in the Gospels, when Jesus was invited to eat at a Pharisee's house. A woman was there who'd been deemed sinful. "A woman in that town who lived a sinful life learned that Jesus was eating at the Pharisee's house, so she came there with an alabaster jar of perfume. As she stood behind him at his feet weeping, she began to wet his feet with her tears. Then she wiped them with her hair, kissed them and poured perfume on them" (Luke 7:37–38). Pretty extravagant, right? We know that this woman made a sacrifice because an alabaster jar was something of high value. But also, she came into an unfamiliar place where she'd be surrounded by Pharisees who would likely judge her for her actions. Yet she chose to be grateful to Jesus for His presence and the gift He gave by seeing her deeply and loving her no less than anyone else. It didn't matter who was watching, what she had to do, or who she was expected to impress. Her presence there showed courage, despite how others labeled her. Later in the story, Jesus declared publicly, in front of the Pharisees, that she was forgiven of her sins.

This woman's life wasn't perfect. She didn't have everything together, and the community around her had labeled her as a "sinner." But her gratitude for the person of Jesus and what He was capable of in her life unlocked something amazing for her. Jesus publicly declared that she was forgiven and free from her sins. Then he charged her to go and live a life knowing that hope was available through Him and that she had the strength to sin no more (vv. 48–50).

I wonder what gratitude looks like in your life right now. I wonder if the weight you're carrying could be lifted and lightened by adopting a simple posture of gratitude. I'm not saying this is a formula for healing, but it is a *tool*. Listen, sis, healing is painful. After walking through a healing journey of my own, and walking with hundreds of women through their own healing journeys, I've come to face the fact that the pain we endure before our healing journeys begin is the pain we'll carry *into* our healing journeys. But transformation takes work. Stronger muscles aren't built without being broken down first. Just like when you're trying to get a fitter body, after a day or two in the gym you're incredibly sore. When you work out, your muscles experience something called *microtears*—essentially tiny tears in the muscles that you've worked. When that happens, your body sends nutrition and blood flow to the area to help it heal. In turn, you grow muscles and become stronger.

The goal of healing is for you to become stronger in your mind, stronger in your heart, and stronger in your spirit. Think of gratitude as your protein shake. It helps your body respond to microtears from deep pain and unhealthy attachments. Gratitude reminds you of where you've come from over the months or days or even years of healing, so you can find the strength to keep going.

THE GOAL OF HEALING IS FOR YOU TO BECOME STRONGER IN YOUR MIND, STRONGER IN YOUR HEART, AND STRONGER IN YOUR SPIRIT.

I want you to be equipped to navigate this journey, and I want to be honest about how difficult it can be to heal. But I promise you, it's worth it. I firmly believe that on the other side of your hard and holy work is a woman who lives her life with grit and hope. That woman is you, and she's stunning. She looks the dark past in the eye, and she says, "You have no more power here. You can't have my future. I will claw my way to hope, and I won't dare give up. I am alive and breathing, and as long as there is breath in my lungs, I will thank God for it. I will use it to create a better future for myself and the people who are connected to me." That is the power of you saying yes to healing and wholeness. And that's real good news!

You have made it this far. What a brave thing you have done. Being willing to do this work takes courage. I'm super proud of you. Now I want us to consider what gratitude looks like daily, how we can include it in our prayers, and what gratitude does for the brain.

GRATITUDE: IT ALL SOUNDS SEXY UNTIL WE HAVE TO DO IT

I remember watching a movie in which parents who were pretty financially well off gave their kid a high-tech, remote-controlled car. It was awesome, but he was so upset because they had gotten him a blue car instead of the red one he wanted. I remember the look on the parents' faces, full of irritation and frustration. They'd gone out of their way to get this toy and even expressed that they stood in a long line to get it, but when they got to the front of the line, the store no longer had red. The son was still upset and even threw the car across the room.

Gosh, we have seen what it looks like for someone to be ungrateful. We cringe. We think, *If that were me I would've been much more grateful than that person*. There's something in us that loves the way gratitude looks. Oprah explained, "The single greatest thing you can do to change your life today would be to start being grateful for what you have right now. And the more grateful you are the more you get."[2]

Doesn't that sound attractive? Gratitude sounds real sexy, but without strategy and intentionality it won't happen in your life. I plan to offer you practical ways to cultivate the weapon of gratitude against the Enemy and be able to access a new level of hope. That's the strategy part. But it's going to be your intentionality that takes you from knowing how to be grateful and accepting that it's an important part of your life to actually practicing gratitude.

Before we dive into these practical strategies, however, I want to warn you about using gratitude in the wrong way. I remember a video call with a few of the women in our course when we were talking through this idea of gratitude. Reflecting, one woman said, "Well, Toni, I agree that gratitude can unlock a lot of good things in our lives, but I feel like there are moments when something disappointing happens in my life and I simply brush it off and make myself remember that I have too many things to be grateful for to be disappointed or upset about something negative that has happened. I find myself saying things like, 'Well it could be worse; get over it. Just be grateful.' How do I stay grateful for the things I have without belittling my pain?"

I loved her question, and I could tell that the other women on the call were interested in my answer by the way they leaned a little closer into their computer screens in anticipation.

I thanked her for asking the question and then explained that gratitude is not a crutch or a Band-Aid; it's a tool for moving forward. We never want to dismiss our disappointments or pain. We are definitely not in the business of stuffing our emotions and sweeping hard things under the rug. Trust me—I've been there, and it never stays under that rug. We always leak. We address and lean into hard things because that's where we build grit and courage. As my friend Karrie Scott Garcia says, "Hope rises from the dirt."[3] It's when we are willing to get dirty and face our hard things that hope comes alive. Hope is about overcoming the valleys. Because we don't dare stay there. We have a saying in our women's ministry: "We'll meet you in the valleys, but we won't leave you there." There's a balance in sitting in the hard and pursuing the holy. I've said it before: hurt and hope can coexist. So when—

GRATITUDE IS ONE OF THE TOOLS YOU CAN USE TO CLAW YOUR WAY OUT OF A VALLEY.

not if—you find yourself in a valley, practice gratitude. Gratitude is one of the tools you can use to claw your way out of a valley.

Let's talk about what gratitude does for your brain. After all, it is the second largest internal organ in your body and it controls your thoughts, which control your feelings, which in turn control your actions. The truth is, we all want to be happy and filled with joy. And when we express our gratitude it not only helps our relationships to grow and be filled with joy, but it also helps us to deal with adversities quicker and with more resilience, and it trains our bodies not to be as negatively affected. Gratitude also pumps happy endorphins through our bodies by producing a positive emotion, which in turn impacts our mental and physical health. A study by psychologist Robert Holden concluded that conditions like anxiety and depression come from a deep root of unhappiness with a part or the totality of our lives.[4] If gratitude can produce positive emotions like happiness, how much more equipped do you think you'll be to withstand the very real effects of things like anxiety and depression?

Gratitude influences our brain on a neurological level because it affects our central nervous system and can act as a natural antidepressant. When you dive into gratitude practices daily, it not only gives you a short-term feeling of happiness, but it produces a long-term happiness and healthy contentment with your life. When we practice gratitude, our brains release chemicals called dopamine and serotonin. Dopamine is a neurotransmitter that sends messages back and forth to your nerve cells. It's responsible for how we feel pleasure and motivation. It's that feeling you get when you complete something hard, and you feel good about it.

Serotonin is a hormone that's used to stabilize our emotions and provide us with safety and happiness. It helps with things like appetite and sleeping. Ever wonder why you have issues with eating when you're nervous or upset? Ever wonder why you have trouble sleeping when you experience big negative emotions? The cause could be a lack of serotonin.[5]

A doctor might even prescribe a selective serotonin reuptake inhibitor (SSRI) to help with depression because it increases the levels of serotonin in your brain. When you practice gratitude, you help to build those two neurotransmitters in your brain. And the more you do it, the more lasting your gratitude, positive energy, and positive behaviors will be.

Not only does gratitude affect your state of being through your brain and its functions, but gratitude is also God's charge to us. Paul wrote to the Christian community in Thessalonica, saying, "Rejoice always, pray continually, give thanks in all circumstances; for this is God's will for you in Christ Jesus" (1 Thessalonians 5:16–18). Paul was clear here: Jesus wants us to be glad, prayerful, and thankful no matter what we're facing. Easier said than done, right? It's easy to thank God when something awesome happens. When we receive something we have longed for. But what about thanking Him in the in-between? What does it look like to say, "God, I am grateful that I woke up today. I am grateful that I have lights. I am grateful that my limbs work"?

Let's go deeper. How difficult is it for you to say things like, "God, I am grateful that relationship didn't work out. You obviously have better for me"? Or, "I am grateful I didn't get that job. I felt like I needed it, but I know You're in charge of all my needs." Or, "That hurt, but, God, I am grateful." Paul also wrote, "Do not be anxious about anything, but in every situation, by prayer and petition, with thanksgiving, present your requests to God" (Philippians 4:6). What does gratitude look like in our lives when we don't get what we want? Can we find the strength in all situations to express gratitude anyway?

Well, I think we can, but it will take practice. And it will take accepting that gratitude is a double blessing for Christians. Not only does gratitude help us neurologically and influence our emotional state, but it also brings us closer in our relationship with God. When we are grateful for the things God has given us, we are thanking the Source. And in our pursuit of a healthy and whole relationship with Him, gratitude toward Him produces intimacy and closeness. It helps us develop endurance and trust in the sovereignty of God. Gratitude keeps us tethered to Him. The truth is, the journey to gratitude won't happen overnight, but when we develop the habits we need and practice them *every* day, small, temporary changes become permanent. And then you'll look up and realize that you've healed and grown in places you wouldn't even have imagined.

I know that was a lot to process. But I think it's important for us to know the gravity of gratitude and how it can shift your life in ways that can create lasting, positive impact. Let's dive into three ways you can begin practicing gratitude in your life daily.

1. Compliment Yourself

One of the things we have a lot of trouble doing as women is complimenting ourselves. Over the years the concept of confidence has been mixed up with pride, which has led to narcissism and a hyperfocus on insecurity. But the truth is, there is a right way to compliment yourself.

When I look back at the moments when pride surfaced in my life because of deeply rooted insecurities, it showed up in the way I used to talk about myself all the time. I'd say things like, "Well, look at what I can do" and "I'm the best at this. Nobody can beat me." In those moments I was looking for validation. I didn't get a lot of praise growing up, so I was casting a net of insecurity, just waiting for someone to tell me I was good and they were proud of me. That side of pride and insecurity can take over. Then I remember when I began to heal and practice humility. I went all the way to the other side. I would talk down to myself and try to become smaller and less than what I was so no one would pay attention to me and I wouldn't fall back on the pride side again.

Then I heard our friend and incredible pastor and leadership coach Jeff Henderson talk about avoiding this pendulum by practicing confident humility. Jeff described it as a beautiful balance of our godly confidence and our human humility.[6] When you find the right balance of confident humility, here's what it looks like: It looks like you being able to compliment yourself and getting to the point where you believe it. Being able to say, "I am strong and resilient, and I can get through this. I am worthy, and there is not one thing in this world that can take away my self-worth. I am a daughter of the King, and hope and redemption belong to me. Healing is something I can actively pursue, and it will come to me."

But it's also being able to say, "I don't have it all figured out, I will make mistakes, and I am guilty of bad choices. Guilt says that I've done something bad, while shame says that I am bad. And I am not bad." Confident humility is a reminder of how you are made in Christ. It's not about what you have, how many likes and followers you have, about how good or fine you look and how sexy you can be. It's about the core—the untouchable, unwavering core of who you are. The core that nobody on this earth can take from you. And it is from that place of confident humility that I want you to practice complimenting yourself.

It may be with words you needed to hear for years that you repeat every single day. You could take a sticky note and put it on your mirror and proclaim good things over your life and your heart every day. You could make a graphic on your computer with your compliments and use it as your background wallpaper, so every day you see those words of confidence.

At one point, my daughter was having difficult behavior issues in school, and her self-confidence was going down. She spiraled into a dark place. Every single morning, I would say, "Dylan, you are smart, you are beautiful inside and out, you are good, you are brave, and you are loved by God, by Jesus, and by your family." Over time I saw a confidence in Dylan that made it easier for her to be grateful for the things that were happening in her life because she first was grateful for her very existence. She even says these things to herself now. "I am smart. I am beautiful inside and out. I am good. I am brave, and Jesus loves me. So does my family." It's so sweet.

Here's a good starting place as you being to compliment yourself in confident humility:

- I may not have it all figured out, but I am capable and strong enough to endure until I do.
- I may experience really hard emotions, but I have the grit needed to process these emotions and return back to hope.
- Even if I get one thing done today, I am crushing it! I am capable of doing hard things.
- I am wildly loved by God. He creates beautiful things, including me.

Don't be shy! Read those out loud, create more for yourself, and lavish yourself with those words in the same way your Creator, God, lavishes you with love.

2. Show and Speak Gratitude to Others

Not only is it important for us to compliment ourselves and be grateful for where we are and who we are, but it is also important to show and speak gratitude to others. Remember, God said it is not good for man to be alone (Genesis 2:18). We need people and the value, substance, and connection that they give us. When we speak gratitude to others, we are reminded about another beautiful gift God has given us, and that's community.

Who can you call or send a text to or tell them in person that you're grateful for them? Can you go a step further and tell them why you're grateful for them? As someone who has been divorced, I don't take for granted that God has given me a new and beautiful marriage, one that I honestly didn't think I deserved and would ever experience. So now I do my best to tell my husband I am grateful for him and I appreciate all that he has done to help restore my sense of love and connection. When I do that, he feels amazing because his love language is words of affirmation. But also, I get overwhelmed with gratitude when I speak it to him because I realize that God gave me a second chance at love. I am more invested in my marriage and the health of it when I recognize the gift it is.

When I tell my daughter I'm grateful to be her mom, it eases the sometimes-hard moments of parenting. My daughter is a gift to me given by God to steward and raise and point in the right direction back to Him. But parenting is no joke! It pushes you to your end in ways that you didn't even know you could experience. But when I look my daughter in the eyes and tell her I'm grateful for her life, that I'm grateful to be her mom, I am more intentional with my temper and my patience with her and with how I raise her.

When I express my gratitude for them, I enjoy my husband and my daughter even more. This same principle can apply to your friends, coworkers, and even pets. Make it a habit to be grateful for someone in your life, but don't just hold it in; tell them. You never know what's on the other side of your words to someone who may need to hear them.

3. Don't Just Say It; Write It, Review It, and Meditate on It

Keeping a journal dedicated to gratitude is a great first step. According to psychologist Martin Seligman, when you write out the things you're grateful for, it has the power to remove stress in your life, improve your sleeping patterns, and even build an awareness of your emotions.[7]

Those first two practices—complimenting yourself and showing and speaking gratitude to others—are opportunities to capture in your journal. You can write them down as a checklist for the day. And you can even follow up and write about how speaking some of those words of confident humility made you feel, or how someone responded when you expressed your gratitude for them. It's important to write these things down not only for the moment but so you can reflect further on them later. I'd recommend choosing a day at the end of the week to read over all the things you've practiced, said, and felt. By taking a moment to pause and look back on what God has done throughout the week, you may be surprised at the ways He is leading you that you might have otherwise missed.

Another great exercise I want to leave you with is a meditation exercise built around gratitude reflection. As you are reviewing the things you've been grateful for in your journal, take a moment to get in a relaxed position, take a few deep breaths, and center yourself. You can start off by saying something like, "I am grateful for this moment." You can also list other things that you're grateful for in that moment. Next I want you to start thinking about those people you're grateful for. You can say to yourself, "I am grateful for my friend. I am grateful for my family member. I am grateful for my children and coworkers." Then I want you to practice turning your attention to yourself and remembering those compliments that spoke to your heart. "I am grateful that I am growing. I am grateful that I am healing and becoming a more whole and holy woman. I am grateful that today I am more hopeful." End your time with another deep breath, and you're done.

I hope these three ways to practice gratitude have helped you find a new outlook on your life and what you do have. I hope this draws you closer to healing and wholeness. I believe it will. You may be excited about starting this practice. But that's not the hard part. The hard part is sticking with it! Set a calendar reminder, find accountability partners, and make this a habit. You deserve it, and the future version of you deserves it as well.

As we transition into part 3 of this book, I want to encourage you to finish well. You have made it through very deep and intentional work, and now it's time for you to discover more about how to develop the grit needed to embrace the pain to find healing and hope.

PART 3

WALKING BRAVELY IN HOPE

You made it to part 3 of the book and this is the part where you can pat yourself on the back. Because right here, in this moment, you can proudly say that you practiced bravery and built grit. This part of the book isn't about you getting a diploma for all the hard work you did, it's about putting on the cutest backpack or satchel with all the tools you've learned so that when you go back to your world, your community, and your relationships, you will show up there as a hopeful woman ready to heal. Let's finish well!

CHAPTER 9

LIVING IN HOPE

WALK IT OUT, SIS!

The summer of my fifth-grade year of elementary school, my parents finally let me go to the neighborhood pool by myself. I was so excited! I would get to walk through the neighborhood to the pool by myself, use my pool pass on my own, and hang out with the other kids without worrying about my parents embarrassing me or telling me it was time to go home. There was one problem: I was a horrible swimmer.

Sharks and Minnows is a fun game where the kids who pretend to be sharks tag the minnows and turn them into sharks until there's only one minnow left and declared the winner. The sharks are on one side of the pool and the minnows have to get to the other side without getting caught. I was determined to play, so I swam over from the shallow end into the deep end and held on to the railing as a minnow. When the sharks started to attack, I doggy paddled my way to the other side of the pool. I was tagged by a shark every single time, and I got tired of losing because of my poor swimming abilities.

As I sat on the benches outside the pool, embarrassed because of how horrible I was at swimming, I came up with an idea. I decided that this was going to be the day I swam underwater. I was going to jump in the deep end and force myself to learn how to swim underwater. No longer would I be afraid. Plus, that's what I saw in the movies. The parent just pushes the kid in and—*boom!*—the kid was swimming.

I grabbed my goggles that covered my eyes and nose, along with my orange pool noodle, and aggressively walked toward the diving board over the deep end of the pool. I waited in line, nervous and uncertain of whether I'd completely fail, but still determined to be a swimmer. It was finally my turn. I wrapped the pool noodle around my legs and body, stood on the diving board, and walked to the edge, one shaking step at a time. And sheer panic came over me. *I couldn't do it*, I thought. *This was a bad idea.* My breathing sped up with each step I took. I made it to the end, bent my knees, and splash. I'd jumped in the pool!

But wait—my pool noodle had flown off and I was swallowing water. I was trying to tread water, but I was choking and freaking out. The lifeguard jumped in the water and pulled me to the edge of the pool to help me get out. I was so embarrassed and defeated I grabbed my things, left the pool, and started walking home. I'll never forget how crushed I was. How bad I felt about failing in front of all those kids. How I had tried but still didn't get what I had hoped for.

Fast-forward to the end of the summer, and I wanted to learn how to ride my bike with no training wheels. Even though I was in the fifth grade and most kids knew how to ride a bike at that age, because my mom had been so sick and my dad worked a lot, I didn't have anyone to teach me in the years when everyone else was learning. I was tired of being the only kid in the neighborhood with training wheels and I was determined to learn how to ride without them.

My dad helped take the wheels off my bike and my mom felt well enough to help me in the front yard on the sidewalk. I'll never forget that white, purple, and pink Barbie bike that I loved. I had my knee and elbow pads and my Barbie helmet on, and I was safe on the sidewalk to fall off and get scuffed up a few times. As my mom encouraged me, I would take off pedaling, then stop because I lost my balance. Then again, and again, and again. Finally, I started pedaling down the sidewalk and didn't have to stop. I did it! I was riding my bike with no training wheels. I was so proud of myself.

What was the difference between that moment of risk and success with my bike and that jump into the deep end of the pool? A lot. When I rode my bike, I had the right tools to keep me safe: my helmet and knee and elbow pads. While jumping into the deep end I had a pool noodle that wasn't at all made to keep me safe. When I rode my bike I stayed on the sidewalk to practice and didn't just go out into the open road like I had jumped into the deep end of the pool. I could have practiced swimming underwater at the shallow end and worked my way up to it, but I got a little too excited. Last, I had a guide when riding my bike. My mom. She was the person who told me to wear my helmet, told me to put my pads on, and guided me to stay on the sidewalk until I felt confident enough to go into the street.

This is where you are now after learning the road map of healing and hope. You're equipped, you've had me as a guide, hopefully you've found a certified counselor if you don't already have one, and you've learned that you are in the safety and presence of a God who is with you the whole way. And now it's time to live in hope. It's time to practice the things you've learned. You have this roadmap, and now it's time to start pedaling on the open road. Don't worry; I won't leave you hanging. Let's talk a little about hope and what it looks like to fully live in it.

It's one thing to define hope from the viewpoint of a human with limited view of the future, but it's got more depth and strength when it's built on a foundation of what God says about hope and how He defines it as the confident expectation of what He has promised. Let's take a moment to read through words of truth when it comes to hope (emphasis added). Words that can't be denied or argued with. Words from our heavenly Father.

"I know the plans I have for you," declares the LORD, "plans to prosper you and not to harm you, plans to give you *hope* and a future." (Jeremiah 29:11)

We wait in *hope* for the LORD; He is our help and our shield. (Psalm 33:20)

May the God of *hope* fill you with all joy and peace in believing, so that by the power of the Holy Spirit you may abound in *hope*. (Romans 15:13 ESV)

"I will make the Valley of Trouble a door of *hope*." (Hosea 2:15 NCV)

God will never forget the needy; the *hope* of the afflicted will never perish. (Psalm 9:18)

Those who *hope* in the LORD will renew their strength. They will soar on wings like eagles; they will run and not grow weary, they will walk and not be faint. (Isaiah 40:31)

Whoo, yes! Those are only six verses out of the more than 150 verses in the Old and New Testaments of the Bible that mention hope. God is serious about our knowing and walking fully in His hope. We can choose to accept that even in the hardest moments of our lives, one thing remains: the hope of Jesus. That's what I want you to know and be bold enough to accept in those hard moments—that God's divine plan for your life includes hope and not harm. That you aren't just waiting *helplessly*. No, you are waiting in hope because the Lord is your shield, and He is protecting you all the way through those valleys. He doesn't just give hope, sis. God *is* hope. And He can take the depths of your troubles and provide a door to hope.

Picking up this book was a door to hope. Not one that I provided to you, but one God Himself planned for you to read and process, reflecting on your own unique story. Will you believe it? Will you believe that God doesn't forget you when you're in need? Do you believe your hope will never wither because God won't let you go? And can you muster up the strength as you're doing the work of healing to place your hope in the Lord and be renewed? That's what our God has to tell you about hope today.

And don't you want to be a hopeful woman? When you interface with someone who walks in the hope of Jesus in the darkest moments, it literally changes you. We've all had that friend, read that story, or watched that video when a woman with a life-threatening disease, a woman who lost a family member, a woman who has experienced abuse is still able to put her faith in Jesus and use her pain to help others. And when we see it, we admire it. Something about it changes us. Those are the people who get the "hopeful" badge. Because they know, no matter what happens, there's hope in a sovereign God who is close and who gives us hope when all seems to be lost.

And now you are claiming hope in your life. You are doing the work, you've walked through chapters on prayer and worship to work on your relationship with God. You've learned about how to do community well and even learned how to nurture healthy relationships and stay away from toxic ones. You've pressed into counseling, which is a scary word for many. But you braved it and even learned some tools to help you play your part in seeking counseling. And you even learned a new daily practice of gratitude.

You've done the work, and now you get to walk that out in your everyday life. You get to be the woman who people look at and say, "Wow, she's got bruised knuckles and a hope she's fought for. She's fighting through all of it, with Jesus leading the way, and she *ain't* giving up!" That is who you are! Claim it! On your couch, in your office, or in your car, say it out loud right now. *"I am a woman of hope!"* I think you can do better than that (unless your kid is sleeping, or your boss can hear you, or your roomie is in the other room and may think something is wrong). Say it again: *"I am a woman of hope!"* That's right, you are. And that's such good news today.

Now that you've claimed it's yours, here's what you can expect while living a life of hope. You can expect for it to be hard in some moments. I know that's not the best thing to read right after you've proclaimed hope. But I'm not here to sell you falsehoods. I'm here to equip you to handle all that life throws your way. Even when hard times come, you can expect to handle them through a lens of hope.

Let's say you suffer a financial loss, whether it is a lost job or a failed business. Instead of allowing the defeat of financial stress and pressure to consume you, living a hopeful life says that you will take this heavy burden to the feet of Jesus, to your safe community, and to your counselor. And you will assess how it has impacted you. You will find healing for those parts of you and you will hold up your head and pursue other means for your financial success.

If you go through a hard breakup, you don't need to spend your days curled up in a ball, crying and calling your ex. Instead of begging to be taken back, producing more wounds of rejection and abandonment, you will take your heartache to the Lover of your soul, your heavenly Father who also freely offers intimacy whenever we need it. You will be able to differentiate between being lonely and being alone. You will know that while being lonely is a real feeling, you are never, ever alone.

When that addiction tempts you and you feel stressed and like it's the only thing that can numb the pain, you will pause and remember that the addiction does not own you and it doesn't have the final say. You will take your anxiety and your pain to Jesus for a permanent fix and not turn to substances for a temporary one. You will remember the way it feels to be whole, to grow, and to have hope for your future.

When depression settles in, and you're feeling isolated and depleted, you will remember that the closer you are to God, the closer you are to joy. When any form of darkness comes into your life, you will remember that the same God who brought you out of it before can and will do it again. Living in hope is not easy, but it's so worth it.

THE LAST KEY TO HOPE

There is one last thing that can keep you from living a life of hope: unforgiveness. I know it's not a fun topic. But when you hold on to the anger and bitterness that comes with not forgiving someone who hurt you, it continues to hurt you. It has power over your thoughts, your actions, and even your faith. And I am not saying the person who hurt you was not wrong. You did not deserve the pain that you endured. But you also don't deserve the bondage of holding on to unforgiveness. I want to encourage you to forgive the people who hurt you, the people who betrayed you, forgive God if you are blaming Him, and maybe even forgive yourself. I want you to look at three aspects of forgiveness as you process your new life of hope.

1. **Your pain does not excuse you from forgiveness.** I know that may be hard to read. But it's true. We all have a responsibility and a reason to forgive. Our responsibility comes from God. Jesus said we should "be merciful, just as your Father is merciful" (Luke 6:36). If we are willing to accept the freely given forgiveness of our Savior, we'd better

be willing to give it away freely as well. When we allow our pain to keep us in a state of unforgiveness, we stay in a victim mindset. And in that victim place we can't access the life-giving oxygen we're calling hope. Instead, we stay wounded, we keep leaking and affecting our other relationships negatively, and we never get to the victory Jesus already claimed for us on the cross.

2. **When we forgive, the grip of bitterness releases our hearts to create a pathway for God to heal us.** Our flesh wants to right wrongs done against us, level the playing field, seek revenge. But God is the ultimate Ruler. He's seen the beginning and the end of the situations and lives of the people who hurt you. He's all-knowing, sovereign, the Judge, *and* the Healer. God is in the business of answered prayers. Jesus said, "Therefore I tell you, whatever you ask for in prayer, believe that you have received it, and it will be yours" (Mark 11:24). What are you going to pray? Prayers that God would punish your offenders and make things fair? Or that He would heal your heart? That God would be close to you during your time of processing? Or that He would work things out without you ever having to lift a finger? We need to focus our energy on God and what He wants to do in our hearts, not against the people who have hurt our hearts.

3. **The Enemy is real.** Remember, we have an Enemy who wants to rob us of our hope, and we need to prepare for that. "Our struggle is not against flesh and blood, but against the rulers, against the authorities, against the powers of this dark world and against the spiritual forces of evil in the heavenly realms" (Ephesians 6:12). Yes, you have an Enemy, and he doesn't isolate his attacks. From relationships to shame and unforgiveness, he is lurking in the spiritual shadows,

whispering thoughts of bitterness and anger that distract you from hope. Your parents, your ex, your old boss, or your faith leader may have hurt you. And again, that hurt is valid. But don't forget who your real Enemy is and where your real battlefields are. Often we are distracted by people from our past who have hurt us, and we forget that the Enemy will attack our weakest places. Unforgiveness is a weak place, so watch it carefully.

Briefly, here's what I want you to remember: when something happens that leaves you feeling like you're in a valley, bring it to God first, seek professional help, bring it to your trusted and safe community, and remember your posture of hope. Remember that you're different now; you're on a different trajectory, and no one can take that from you. You are a woman of hope. Wear that badge proudly, and let's get prepared to go to battle.

CHAPTER 10

A HOLY TINGLE

KEEPING YOUR EYE ON THE REAL ENEMY

My daughter Dylan does a very interesting thing when she is attempting something she's afraid of. It could be climbing heights, grabbing a bug, riding her bike, or even jumping into the pool. She starts out afraid. I give her encouragement, show her how to do it, and, if needed, bribe her with a reward. Typically she succeeds, and then she does it over and over again and all is well. But something curious happens when, after time passes, she goes back to do it again. She's completely afraid like she was the first time. I'm not kidding; it's as if she's forgotten that she was already scared, already overcame it, and had a great time. I think she simply forgets. When fear creeps into her little heart, it takes over her thoughts, which then take over her feelings and ultimately take over her actions. And she has to be encouraged and bribed all over again.

I think that's how the Enemy of our soul gets us. He inflicts fear, and we forget how strong we are and how far we've come. I can remember early moments in my marriage when I would get triggered. Whether it was something I did or something my husband said or a circumstance that came up with my ex-husband, I would just crumble. *Am I going to fail again? Is the anxiety coming back? Will he leave me? Did the counseling not work? Has God left me?* I remember those thoughts—those lies swirling around in my mind, paralyzing me, bringing up doubts and ultimately bad actions when I believed them.

And then I learned that when those types of thoughts come into my brain, that is a sure sign of the Enemy. He is the author of lies and confusion. And when negative thoughts about myself, my life, and my healing come into my brain, I know now that they are not from God. God doesn't speak to our hearts in that way. That's the

Enemy's work. The strength beneath the lies of the Enemy is that he bullies us into believing we are the only ones who have felt broken. When really, every daughter, friend, teacher, lawyer, leader, cousin, aunt, and woman you know each has her own type of brokenness. But when brokenness partners up with the comparison trap, it tells us everyone else is doing better than we are, that we are completely alone in feeling lost, stuck, or empty. The Enemy also tells us that this dark night will last forever. He likes to trap us into thinking that nothing will ever be able to touch our brokenness and make us whole or hopeful ever again. And maybe the most dangerous, heartbreaking lie he whispers to us is that the heaviness we are carrying could never be understood by our heavenly Father. But those are all lies. And we will not stand for them. You need to be prepared to combat those lies with truth.

THE STRENGTH BENEATH THE LIES OF THE ENEMY IS THAT HE BULLIES US INTO BELIEVING WE ARE THE ONLY ONES WHO HAVE FELT BROKEN.

One of the things I often hear from women is that they know God, they believe in His power, but everything is still so hard. I've been there. I've felt like I was close to God and was following Him with a pure heart but still felt crushed by life and defeated. What if it's not only about knowing God, but it's also about knowing the Enemy well enough to recognize his schemes, be prepared for how he'll attack, and have the right tools in place to defend your mind, heart, and spirit?

The Enemy attacks in three ways. It's not that hard to see them once you know them. He's so predictable. The big three are:

You are unworthy.
You are less than others.
You don't need help.

Let's dig into all three.

UNWORTHINESS

The first lie the Enemy will whisper to try to defeat you is that you are unworthy. Unworthy of love, peace, hope, and a beautiful life. Why? To better understand his lies, let's examine who Satan is.

Satan was known as God's most beautiful angel. He was one of the first and most honored angels.

> You were anointed as a guardian cherub,
> for so I ordained you.
> You were on the holy mount of God;
> you walked among the fiery stones.
> You were blameless in your ways
> from the day you were created
> till wickedness was found in you.
> Through your widespread trade
> you were filled with violence,
> and you sinned.
> So I drove you in disgrace from the mount
> of God,
> and I expelled you, guardian cherub,
> from among the fiery stones.

(Ezekiel 28:14–16)

The Lord had given Satan, then called Lucifer, the gift of music and voice. God didn't create him as evil. He created something good, an angel. But Satan turned evil. And you know how? *Pride.* Satan started to believe too highly of himself. He swung way toward the side of pride because of all the gifts he had. He wanted the honor that only belonged to God. He wanted it so bad, he was willing to battle God for it. Of course, he didn't win, and according to Revelation 12, he was cast out of heaven and took with him the angels that chose to follow him. And now, Satan and his "fallen" angels want to defeat us here on earth.

Reese Bricken, a leader of Feminine Hearts Alive, stood on stage at the spiritual encounter and said that one of the ways Satan attacks us as women is through our beauty. Both inside and out. Aren't we the ones called beautiful? In Song of Solomon 4:7, the writer says about a woman, "You are altogether beautiful, my darling; there is no flaw in you." I mean, we are just marvelous.

Think about this for a moment. God created the earth and moon and stars. He created every animal and the places where the water meets the land. He filled up the dark chaos with beautiful hues and living creatures of every kind. Then He created Adam, a strong, resilient protector of the land. And yet . . . He wasn't done. All those things were glorious. But He wasn't finished until He made you and me. Remember, the world wasn't complete until He made woman. We are the period to earth's creation. We are the final stroke of the glorious workmanship of God. That's you and me.

And so yes, Satan was upset, and he made his move in the garden with Eve. Taunting her, confusing her into believing that she needed to eat from the Tree of Knowledge of Good and Evil.

Now the serpent was more crafty than any of the wild animals the LORD God had made. He said to the woman, "Did God really say, 'You must not eat from any tree in the garden'?"

The woman said to the serpent, "We may eat fruit from the trees in the garden, but God did say, 'You must not eat fruit from the tree that is in the middle of the garden, and you must not touch it, or you will die."

"You will not certainly die," the serpent said to the woman. "For God knows that when you eat from it your eyes will be opened, and you will be like God, knowing good and evil." (Genesis 3:1–5)

He knew just how to get her. He attacked her worth. She must have thought, *Well, why wouldn't God give me access to good and evil? Why wouldn't He want me to know? Does He not love me? Does He not think I deserve to know?* And it worked. She turned from God to access what she felt would make her have wisdom like God. Little did Eve understand that she was worthy of something far greater than even knowledge and power. She was worthy of the safety and protection of the Creator of all things. That's what is given to you, daughter. Thankfully, when you have been redeemed by Jesus, you are in the safe hands of your heavenly Father. Please know that when insecurity rears its incredibly ugly head and the Enemy tries to tell you that you're not worthy, you can look and recognize who is speaking.

COMPARISON

Second, the Enemy will lead you into the comparison trap. My good friend and pastor Sandra Stanley has a study called *Comparison Trap*. Here's what she says:

From the first time we complain to Mom at the family dinner table that "it's not fair" when our sister gets a bigger slice of dessert, we're constantly looking to our left and to our right to see how we measure up to those around us. Sometimes we come up short—she's skinnier, funnier, or smarter. Sometimes we come out on top—our house is bigger, fancier, or cleaner. But this game of comparison is a game with no winners. There is simply no win in comparison. It brings envy, jealousy, pride, and arrogance. It leads us to make unwise financial decisions just to keep up with those around us. It stains our friendship with gossip and striving. Let's decide today to stop playing the game of comparison—it's a game you simply can't win.[1]

So good, right? But the Enemy will try to draw us into a comparison trap with other people and even worse, other women. He will convince us that we should have what someone else has, that God is withholding something from us that He's given to someone else. The Enemy will whisper that we deserve to be further along, doing more, with more followers and comments and likes, and that God is not good and doesn't want us to succeed. To combat the lies of the Enemy, you've got to be closely tethered to God. You have to know without a doubt that God has good in store for you. And when you hold a posture of humility that says, "God, whatever You want, whenever You want it, I trust in You," the Enemy cannot convince you to compare. And let's be honest— God's way has always been the best way. Satan has a track record of losing, and God's Word of truth tells us that He knows the plans He has for us. And guess what? They are plans to prosper us and not harm us—plans that

> **TO COMBAT THE LIES OF THE ENEMY, YOU'VE GOT TO BE CLOSELY TETHERED TO GOD.**

will last through our hard moments right now, well into the future (Jeremiah 29:11).

INDEPENDENCE AND PERFECTIONISM

Finally, Satan will tempt you to deny you need help. One of the common misconceptions we fall into as women is believing that we have to do everything ourselves. We get into a mode where we feel like we have to stuff our emotions down so we can be seen as brave and strong. We've all had that moment when someone has asked us how everything was going and instead of telling the truth, we lied. "Oh, everything is going just fine. I'm okay." Why did we do that? Well, I think it is because the world has taught us that to be useful we have to be perfect. We've believed the Enemy's lie that perfection is the key to success.

I am here to tell you that the key to success is not perfection; it's *surrender*. It's being able to lay our burdens at the feet of Jesus and say, "I can't do this alone. I am weak in this area. I am tired. I am weary and confused and disappointed and just defeated." When we get honest with the way we are feeling, we open ourselves up to trade our weakness for God's power. When the Enemy convinces us we don't need help, we shut ourselves off from the power of God. We limit our access to the very thing Jesus died on the cross for: our victory and our triumph over darkness and despair.

And doesn't it make sense that the Enemy wants us to stay shut off and hidden from our heavenly Father? It's so simple for him to do. All he has to do is say that you don't need help and you're stronger because of it. That one little lie can lead to so much destruction. Don't let it. David wrote of God, "You keep track of all my sorrows. You have collected all my tears in your bottle. You have recorded each one in your book" (Psalm 56:8 NLT). Can you believe that? There is a God in heaven who has seen and kept track of all your sorrows. From the little ones to the big ones. And not only that, but He has collected and held close your tears. Not because He is keeping a count of your failures, but because He cherishes your beautiful heart and wants you to know that He is with you.

I remember talking about this in group therapy. Can you imagine that sacred moment when God comes and rescues us from this world and we get to heaven and see Him for the first time? Imagine if you looked at all the tears you cried while you were on earth that He's kept track of. The time you fell down as a little girl and scraped your leg. The first lost friendship that devastated you. Your first heartbreak. When a loved one passed away. Not making the cheerleading or sports team that you wanted to be on. Finding out about an illness in your body. Standing in church and worshipping God for the first time and weeping. Every single one of those moments, you and God will reflect on together, and you will see His tender heart for you in everything that you've been through—how He's been storing your tears up, awaiting your arrival to come closer to Him. That's the God the Enemy wants to keep us away from.

Here are some examples of lies the Enemy will try to use against you:

You're not worth protecting.
You're not worth loving.
You're not worth sticking around for.
You're not enough.
You're broken.
God doesn't care about your pain.
You're an embarrassment.
You're too weak to make it through this.

TRUTH AGAINST LIES

After you have clearly understood the character traits of the Enemy and how he attacks you with lies, you have to replace those lies with ultimate truth. If you're in a season of fighting lies I want you to use this Truth Against Lies template. It's an easy three-step journaling prompt.

1. Identify the Source of the Lie

Go to God in prayer and ask Him to help you identify where the Enemy has fed you lies that you have accepted. Ask God where he has tried to attack your worth. Where has he trapped you into comparison? And where is he convincing you to deny help from God?

2. Notice the Thoughts That Lie Introduces

Listen intently and identify the lies as God speaks to your heart. Typically, as we've learned, they are thoughts that bring destruction to you and your relationships. They're typically negative and full of doubt, and they keep you from being fully hopeful.

3. Capture the Thoughts by Writing Them Down

As they begin to come to your mind, step three is to write them down in your journal. Don't hold back. Be honest with yourself. I know it's hard, but there's no shame in admitting that you have an Enemy who is planting lies in your head. We all do! You're just brave enough to address them so they have no power over you.

Understanding God's truth is important because it helps us build foundations of beliefs to stand on when lies try to fill our hearts and minds. In our women's course, we write out the following statement about accessing God's truth. You may want to copy it into your journal.

No matter how loud or believable the voice of the Enemy can be in our lives, he is a liar. We know based on the life of Jesus that He mourned with those who were sitting in the middle of loss. When Lazarus died, Jesus wept with Lazarus's sisters, wept over the death of His friend. Our God is a God who gets down into the pit with us to weep with us, mourn with us, grieve with us; He is not a God who stands up at the top of the hole life seems to throw us into and waits for us to fight our way back up to Him. No, our God already made the great trade when Jesus died on the cross: He promises that in all things He will put on our broken-ness and replace it with His wholeness and His strength. And that is where our hope can start: the biggest, most crippling lie the Enemy waves in our face has already been defeated by a Father who stepped off His throne down into the brokenness. Our God is in the business of stepping into the brokenness. He is not afraid of the dark. And He wants us to walk boldly in that truth.

The lies we tell ourselves have damaged us, made us afraid, shamed us, ruined relationships, and left us crushed. But God hasn't left us there. There's no greater way to combat lies the Enemy wants us to believe, that lead to our destruction, than injecting the truth of our Father into our minds, hearts, and ultimately our souls. So start injecting truth.

The Enemy does not have the final say here. He simply does not. I want to challenge you as we are heading into our very last chapter to find the grit you need to push back against the Enemy. And know this: you are not carrying the battle alone. God defeated him once, and He will answer our prayers to defeat him again.

So let God work his will in you. Yell a loud *no* to the Devil and watch him make himself scarce. Say a quiet *yes* to God and he'll be there in no time. Quit dabbling in sin. Purify your inner life. Quit playing the field. Hit bottom and cry your eyes out. The fun and games are over. Get serious, really serious. Get down on your knees before the Master; it's the only way you'll get on your feet. (James 4:7–10 THE MESSAGE)

Our struggle is not always with flesh and blood; it is also against the powers of a dark world (Ephesians 6:12). And if you are going to fight the Enemy, it won't require intellect; it will demand your kneeling. Let's get serious, sister—real serious about our healing. As always, you deserve it.

CHAPTER 11

HOPEFUL WOMAN

STANDING IN THE VALLEYS UNTIL EVERYONE IS OUT

Well, you made it to the last chapter of this journey. Can you believe it? I am so proud of you. I am proud of you for pressing into the hard things. I'm proud of you for not looking back at your past, allowing it to define you and hold you back from everything God has for you. I hope you feel that way about yourself as well. And I hope you know that when you close this book it'll always be there to help guide you back to a life of hope.

For our last chapter, I want to talk about a woman who made some hard decisions for all the right reasons. It may be tough to read, but at this point we can all sit in the hard parts of our stories and hold space for hope. Let's lean in.

This enslaved woman was born in Maryland around 1820 and worked as a cook on a plantation. She had eight brothers and sisters, but many of them were separated despite her attempts to keep them all together. She had a heart to help others and was involved in a terrible accident at twelve years old where she was hit in the head with a heavy weight while protecting someone else from being attacked. The injury caused her a lot of headaches and narcolepsy. She bounced around from plantation to plantation as a nursemaid and was beaten if the children cried.

For a time she worked as a planter to set muskrat traps and was later given a position as field hand. In 1840 she discovered that her father had been set free, and in the plantation owner's will she was also freed, along with her children. Unfortunately, the new owner refused to recognize the will and kept her and her children as slaves.

Around 1844, she began to plan her escape along with her two brothers, and she prevailed. Her brothers were afraid, though, and returned to the plantation. Just as we saw the Israelites admit to Moses that they were afraid and wanted to go back into bondage under Pharaoh's rule, there were slaves who were so afraid of being caught and treated worse that they simply went back. Many slaves couldn't fathom a life on their own. With no education and no finances, they felt safer in bondage. On September 17, 1849, however, this woman escaped and became free. She found a job in Philadelphia as a housekeeper, but there was something stirring in her heart that she just couldn't shake. She didn't feel settled.

Instead of staying in Philadelphia, this woman, who we know as Harriet Tubman, chose to return to the southern part of the United States to free her niece and her nieces' children, using the Underground Railroad. Her own children couldn't be freed because their owners placed a financial price on their freedom that Harriet was unable to pay. During the next ten years, she established the Underground Railroad network, and it is reported that she freed hundreds of people. She claimed, "I never ran my train off the track, and I never lost a passenger."[1] I believe Harriet knew that freedom is best experienced with other people.

Sure, it's a relief to experience freedom and hope for yourself, but when you reach back to help bring others forward, it activates a greater purpose in your life. I believe there are two reasons God saw fit to have you pick up and read this book. One is so you could stand proudly as a brave woman of hope and proclaim victory over your brokenness. Second, I believe God wants to use you to help other women. I believe God's plan was to rescue you, restore you, and equip you to help others be restored as well.

David Kessler is an expert on grief and loss. I heard him speak on what he calls the sixth stage of grief, and it was fascinating.[2] Kessler suffered a tragic loss when his twenty-one-year-old son suddenly passed away. He explained that the five stages of grief, established in

1969 by Elisabeth Kubler-Ross, are denial, anger, bargaining, depression, and acceptance. Those five stages are organic and not succinct. They can happen sporadically and in no particular order. As we know, healing isn't linear. Kessler says that when people are in this cycle they end up feeling stuck and turn to coping mechanisms like addictions, unhealthy relationships, and unhealthy attachments.

He talked about his discomfort with simply accepting grief. He believed there had to be more than sitting in the reality of deep pain and loss. He toyed with the idea of a sixth step to the grief cycle—*meaning*. It could be a way out of feeling so stuck in grief. And while he doubted that it would do anything for the pain, it did. He said, "Meaning didn't take the pain away, but it gave it a cushion. It gave it a companion."

He later received permission from the Kubler-Ross family and foundation to add this sixth step to the official grief cycle because it was recognized as a behavior that did help people feel less stuck in their pain. So adding the sixth step was a real accomplishment! Kessler isn't saying that there's meaning to be found in death or divorce or abuse; rather, the meaning we all search for externally is really found internally. Kessler realized that he wanted to help others process grief and hard loss. It didn't make losing his son hurt less, but it created a pathway for hope in another area in his life.

When we begin to take the very thing that tried to break us and use it to build a life of meaning and purpose, we become alive and feel less alone in our pain. How do I know? Hello! This book is the result of my seeking meaning and purpose from the shards of my own story of loss and healing. I can remember the moment I first stood on a stage and talked about my pain. I was mid-divorce, transitioning from my toxic church, with no job and a daughter I needed to take care of. I was so afraid and confused, but I was scheduled to preach at a middle school youth service. I asked God for help writing the message, and I remember scrolling on Instagram and stumbling upon a graphic that said, "Broken Crayons Still Color." I used that and 2 Corinthians 12:9 to talk about brokenness and how to find hope again even when things suck.

I cried my heart out on that stage, and I'm sure those middle schoolers thought I was crazy. But God showed up like I never had seen Him before. As time went on and I presented that message on stage after stage, visiting my counselor weekly, finding new and healthy community, and just being grateful for where I was, I began healing and growing at a rapid rate. It wasn't about just my life anymore. I got to help others find hope, and that gave me meaning. It created a brand-new pathway for hope and restoration. It didn't change my story, and it surely didn't change the hard work of healing I had to do from my story. It created another way to experience joy and fulfillment in my life.

I couldn't stop there, so I created the organization Broken Crayons Still Color. We know other women are out there in valleys thinking that their brokenness discounts them. And yet there are stories all throughout the Bible showing broken people, including broken women, who God empowers to do life-changing, world-shaking things. I vowed to tell that truth to as many women as possible. And I have seen women's lives change and transform into testimonies of hope in ways I couldn't even pray for. Now I stop at nothing to make sure that every woman I meet knows that hope is available to her even in the most broken places of her life.

Think about Moses and what he and his brother Aaron were tasked to do. Moses lived a stable life in the palace of Pharaoh. He was raised as an Egyptian even though he was an Israelite, and he had a very comfortable life growing up. He didn't have to listen to God's request to set the Israelites free from Pharaoh's bondage, but he did. Exodus 5 details their story.

Moses and Aaron went to Pharaoh and said, "This is what the LORD, the God of Israel, says: 'Let my people go, so that they may hold a festival to me in the wilderness.'"

Pharaoh said, "Who is the LORD, that I should obey him and let Israel go? I do not know the LORD and I will not let Israel go."

Then they said, "The God of the Hebrews has met with us. Now let us take a three-day journey into the wilderness to offer sacrifices to the LORD our God, or he may strike us with plagues or with the sword."

But the king of Egypt said, "Moses and Aaron, why are you taking the people away from their labor? Get back to your work!" Then Pharaoh said, "Look, the people of the land are now numerous, and you are stopping them from working." (vv. 1–5)

Moses, while afraid and unsure of his leadership, stopped at nothing to help his people escape. And through many trials, he was successful. This wasn't about Moses; it was about his helping God fulfill His larger plan to free His people. God wants to equip you to free other women to live a life of healing and wholeness. What if you could speak the one sentence to a woman that would change her life forever? What if it was your story, your brokenness, and your redemption that set someone free to live in hope? Wouldn't you tell your story? Wouldn't you reach back and give a woman hope?

MY HOPE FOR YOU

When I went through my divorce, I wanted to heal and then make sure that I helped other women feel less alone about their divorces. So I wrote a letter. I had a desire that every woman walking through what I clawed my way through would feel less alone in her brokenness by reading it. When I prayed about what letter I wanted to write, I thought about twenty-four-year-old Toni who had just been divorced and had no one to help her through it. I used the very longing that I had in a season of deep hurt and turned it into hope for other women. I want to share my letter with you. I pray as you read it you will see how God is using that story to offer hope to others. And my prayer is that it will inspire you to figure out what words you can share about your healing journey with others.

Hey gal,

Let me just first say this: your divorce doesn't define you. It may have broken you, shattered your dreams of love, left you abused, afraid, broke, alone, lifeless, anxious, and may have robbed you of the life you hoped and dreamed for. It may have told you that you're incapable of giving and receiving love. That maybe something about you is just so broken that a deep and intimate love is impossible for you.

But it doesn't get to define you.

This isn't a dismissal of how it impacted you. I know that pain, deeply. I know what it feels like to pray secret prayers for the person you know your spouse can be. I know what it feels like to be afraid for your emotional and physical well-being at the hand of the person who is supposed to care for you. I know what it feels like to lose the community that you were once connected to. I know what it feels like to have to break it to your kid that you really tried, but the marriage just fell short, and things will look different. I know what it feels like to have the church, who is supposed to help you win, label you a failure.

But divorce doesn't get to define you. Who you are is a daughter held in the arms of the Father (Psalm 34:18). Who you are is a woman God draws close to (James 4:8). Who you are is a woman with the power of God pumping through her veins (2 Corinthians 12:9).

You don't have to carry around the shame of failure. God is not at the end of the tunnels of your life waiting for you to get "cleaned up." He's undoubtedly wiping every tear and broken place, and mending your sweet heart back together again. He still has a hope and future for you (Jeremiah 29:11).

Because divorce doesn't get to define you.

So drop that "divorcee" badge and trade it for "hopeful." You are here now, starting over, proving your resilience, fighting, and clawing your way to a better future, a life of peace, and maybe one day another chance at redeeming love.

Here's to a new start.

Seeing you deeply,

Toni

That letter was an indication of the healing and hope I didn't have before. I couldn't empower women while I was still broken from divorce; I needed to get on the other side and find hope for myself before I could offer it to others. So before we go, I want to offer you two final things I hope will equip you to go out and share the good news of what you've experienced here.

HEAL FIRST

First, it is very important that you heal before you help. We can tell that a woman is still healing by her actions and her words. Typically, when a woman isn't yet healed, her actions and words come from a place of resentment, sadness, and bitterness. But when a woman is healed she produces life-bearing fruit. She shows empathy and grace. It's not to say that she has to forget the pain she's endured, but you can smell the sweet aroma of forgiveness all over her.

That's how you want to represent God. You want people to be able to look at you, glean from you, and be encouraged to go on their own healing journeys. So heal first. Go to counseling and dive into the hard things and do the work. Transition out of toxic relationships and environments that create more trauma for you. Practice gratitude so your mind is pointing forward toward a life of thankfulness and happiness.

IT IS VERY IMPORTANT THAT YOU HEAL BEFORE YOU HELP.

Establish your rhythm with God. God doesn't just want people who know how to repeat all the scriptures they've memorized. We've all seen those types of Jesus-followers. The type that can tell you where a verse is in the Bible but haven't taken the time to sit with a counselor to process through their childhood wounds. God wants holy and healthy and whole people. Because those are the people He can trust with the hearts of His daughters. So check in with yourself and know without a doubt that you are in a stable place so that you can stand firm in the valleys and protect the women assigned to you.

FOLLOW GOD'S LEAD

Second, you need to know who is assigned to you. I remember when I first met my second husband, Sam, I was on the phone all the time. I was either texting or calling my mentees from my student ministry days. Sam, out of curiosity, kept asking who I was spending so much time with. I told him I had four mentees I was trying to pour into. He looked at me in complete shock. We both knew that I was definitely not in a healed state and I was pouring out from a very empty cup. He also was concerned that I wasn't called by God to be caring for all of them. I started to ask myself, *How do I know if I'm called to them?* That's when I started asking God the question, "Are You calling me to care for this person?"

Since then, anytime someone messages me on social media or emails me or even asks me in person about mentoring them or helping them make a decision, I always ask God if He is calling me to that person. I want to encourage you to do the same. God knows the things you are strong in and the things that you are weak in. In this season He may be calling you to someone who has a problem you've already healed from. But a person may come around and be struggling with something you haven't healed from, and you may not be ready to lead that person. And that's okay. We aren't called to everyone. And we don't have to say it in a mean or negative way. When you are in alignment with God and being 100 percent obedient to what He has called you to, and called you from, you're in the best place you can be.

I still can't believe we're at the end of this book. As we close, I'd like to offer up my best to you. A prayer.

> *Dear God, thank You for the life of Your daughter. I don't know what she's been through, and I don't know what deep grief and sorrow she's carrying around and processing. But You do. You've bottled up every single one of her tears and even now in this moment You are watching over her, protecting her, and showing her new ways to hope through healing.*

Lord, I pray You would be close in times when she's feeling brokenhearted and crushed in spirit. I pray You would be so near that she would hear Your voice and listen to the impressions You're placing on her heart. I pray that she would be brave enough to be absolutely broken in the safe place that is Your arms. And I pray You would provide redemption and restoration to her heart.

Lord, I pray You would bring her to a place of healing that allows her to share her story and the good news she now knows: that hope is available to us all.

It's in Jesus' name I pray, amen.

Goodbye for now, hopeful woman. You did it! Remember, no one and nothing can take away the hope that lives inside you. And, with the power of Jesus, you are stronger than your brokenness.

ACKNOWLEDGMENTS

My personal journey to a life of healing and wholeness almost broke me. I didn't think I'd make it to see today, to see writing this book. And, wow, here I am. Not perfect, not without pain, but holding the broken parts of my imperfect humanity with grit and hope.

I didn't get here alone, though.

I got here with my husband, Sam, being one of the first people to tell me that my life still has a purpose greater than I could imagine.

I got here watching my mom fight for her life and living through the redemption of my relationship with my father.

I got here with the Broken Crayons Still Color team, watching them be willing to stand in the trenches for women as they heal. Proving that what God had put on the inside of me for his daughters actually helps.

I got here because I couldn't let my daughter, Dylan, and son, Sam Jr., down.

I got here because of my community of fearless women, marching alongside me, holding my arms up.

And of course . . . I'm still here because of Jesus. His love for me and His sacrifice for my broken life reminds me that bravery can look imperfect and that I'm never alone in the valleys. I hope this book reminds you of the same.

RESOURCES

TIPS FOR FINDING A THERAPIST

Finding the right therapist is important to your healing journey. And while it may seem completely overwhelming, you can do it. Here are some of my tips on how to find a therapist.

Call Your Insurance Provider

Your insurance provider may have in-network options for you to explore. While it may be a small list, it's a great place to start when you're trying to find therapy within a budget. There may also be an option to pay for an out-of-network counselor, submit it to your insurance, and be reimbursed.

Phone a Friend

Most of the counselors I've gone to have been referred by a trusted friend. While some of my friends have had different needs for a counselor, it's been helpful to learn about the therapist's style, demeanor, and abilities from someone I know who's interacted with them before.

Check on the Resources in Your Community

If you're a college student, you may want to check a counseling center in or near your college. If you're employed, check in with your job about an employee assistance program. There may also be options at your church or at a local community center that has a focus on advocacy for harder topics like abuse and trauma.

Get Specific

You may be battling with something very specific like anxiety, depression, suicidal ideation, and intrusive thoughts. Addiction or eating disorders may be a part of your story. And now that you've found the bravery to be honest about those things, it may be beneficial to connect with national organizations that specialize in those topics.

Here's a list of a few trusted organizations:
- National Center for PTSD
- Depression and Bipolar Support Alliance
- National Suicide Prevention Lifeline
- Narcotics Anonymous
- Sexaholics Anonymous
- International OCD Foundation
- GriefShare
- Postpartum Support International
- National Eating Disorders Association
- Black Mental Health Alliance
- Therapy for Latinx
- The National Asian American Pacific Islander Mental Health Association
- RAINN (National Sexual Assault Hotline)

Try Online

COVID wreaked havoc on our entire world, and at the same time it created the ability for us to connect online for the right reasons. Online therapy engines have been refined and reimagined. If you don't feel comfortable with meeting in person just yet, online may be a great option for you.

Here's a list of online therapy platforms:

- Betterhelp.com
- Talkspace.com
- GoodTherapy.com

Don't Exclude Your Faith

One thing that has been plaguing the Christian faith for years is the separation of our faith and our feelings. Both can coexist. So, when you're looking at counseling options, lean into finding someone who will incorporate Christianity into their practice. Many online platforms have a religious filter on them. Don't be afraid to choose a filter that clearly describes what you're looking for!

SCRIPTURES TO LEAN ON

There are moments in our lives when we just need a reminder that God is with us and for us. Come back to these scriptures when you need them, as often as you need them. God's Word never wavers or fails, even in our hardest moments.

Feeling anxious?

Do not be anxious about anything, but in every situation, by prayer and petition, with thanksgiving, present your requests to God. (Philippians 4:6)

Feeling stressed?

"I am leaving you with a gift—peace of mind and heart. And the peace I give is a gift the world cannot give. So don't be troubled or afraid." (John 14:27 NLT)

Feeling weak?

He said to me, "My grace is sufficient for you, for my power is made perfect in weakness." Therefore I will boast all the more gladly about my weaknesses, so that Christ's power may rest on me. (2 Corinthians 12:9)

Feeling unprepared?

The LORD himself goes before you and will be with you; he will never leave you nor forsake you. Do not be afraid; do not be discouraged. (Deuteronomy 31:8)

Feeling afraid?

God is love. When we take up permanent residence in a life of love, we live in God and God lives in us. This way, love has the run of the house, becomes at home and mature in us, so that we're free of worry on Judgment Day—our standing in the world is identical with Christ's. There is no room in love for fear. Well-formed love banishes fear. Since fear is crippling, a fearful life—fear of death, fear of judgment—is one not yet fully formed in love. (1 John 4:17–18 THE MESSAGE)

Feeling heartbroken?

> The LORD is close to the brokenhearted
>> and saves those who are crushed in spirit.
>>> (PSALM 34:18)

Feeling betrayed?

The LORD himself will fight for you. Just stay calm. (Exodus 14:14 NLT)

Feeling alone?

Truly my soul finds rest in God;
> my salvation comes from him.

Truly he is my rock and my salvation;
> he is my fortress, I will never be shaken.
>> (PSALM 62:1–2)

Feeling doubtful?

Have I not commanded you? Be strong and courageous. Do not be afraid; do not be discouraged, for the LORD your God will be with you wherever you go. (Joshua 1:9)

Feeling spiritually attacked?

> Yell a loud *no* to the Devil and watch him make himself scarce. Say a quiet *yes* to God and he'll be there in no time. (James 4:7–8 THE MESSAGE)

GRATITUDE PRACTICES

Gratitude is an incredible practice to help change your thoughts, emotions, and ultimately how you live your life, but it takes intentionality and consistency. Check out these gratitude practices.

Create a Gratitude Jar

Find a jar you love and put it in a place where you see it daily. Put small pieces of paper and a pen next to it, and each time you pass the jar and think of something to be grateful for, write it down, and put it in the jar. When you're feeling down or upset, go to the jar, grab a few notes, and read them for encouragement.

Include Gratitude in Journaling

When you journal, make it a practice to write one to three things you're grateful for before you begin. This can reset your posture going into your time with God and reset your heart as you draw near to Him.

Create a Gratitude Object

This object can be a rock, a marble, a special coin, or anything small you can keep in your purse, wallet, desk area, or pocket. Anytime you encounter the object, try to think of something you're grateful for and say it aloud. You never know when your gratitude object will show up on a day you need it the most!

Seven Days of Intentional Gratitude

A good way to reset if you're going through a particularly hard season is to spend intentional time practicing gratitude using daily prompts for seven days. Every day choose one or more prompts to journal about.

Prompt examples:

- I'm grateful for these three people:
- I'm grateful for these three things in my home:
- I'm grateful for these three lessons I learned:
- I'm grateful for these three scriptures:
- I'm grateful for these three things on my body:
- I'm grateful for these three experiences:
- I'm grateful for these three songs:

Gratitude Stroll

Maybe you're not able to voice the things you're grateful for right now. Instead, how about going for a stroll and focusing your mind on things you're grateful for? All you'll need is a quick ten- to fifteen-minute stroll, being mindful of all you are grateful for.

FIVE TIPS FOR TRANSITIONING OUT OF A TOXIC COMMUNITY

You are worthy of good friendships. You are worthy of being treated and loved well. And, while we are all broken people in need of grace and acceptance, there are some people who cannot have access to your heart because of the potential damage they could do. Remember, you become who you're around. So ask God to be with you in this process, put on your big-girl pants, acknowledge that this is hard but sacred work, and let's go protect your heart.

1. Identify Your Friendship Needs

Create healthy friendship pathways by first identifying your needs in a friendship—the needs that give you life and safety and love. In Ephesians 4 Paul talked about a way to communicate to people that hits their needs both actual and felt. This means that we all have things we need in order to thrive in relationships with others. What are yours?

2. Create and Identify Circles

Even Jesus had circles. Peter, James, and John experienced things the other disciples did not. They were typically listed first in Scripture, and they were absolutely the closest to Jesus. In your circles, think: What level of friendship should this person be in?

3. Identify Toxicity

The Bible makes it clear here; bad company ruins good character (1 Corinthians 15:33). We truly do become who we hang around with, and knowing that we are only responsible for ourselves when we get to heaven, we have to put ourselves in healthy relationships so we can become and be that for others. What toxic behavior, from name-calling to gaslighting, have you recognized in some of your friends?

4. Create Boundaries

Even Jesus set boundaries to protect His heart and sacred spaces. And now we get to create boundaries that are strong enough to keep the bad stuff out and permeable enough to let the good stuff in. What boundaries are you going to set for your friendships? From not allowing harsh words to refusing toxic behaviors, boundaries are healthy for maintaining wholeness.

5. Have an Honest Conversation

A hard conversation is not the end of a relationship, but a new beginning to a friendship that isn't toxic but is resolved in grace and truth. Go into this conversation knowing where you think this person should be placed in your life. Are they moving from intimate to inner? From level two, closest to your heart, or level three? Last, pray about how God would want you to have the conversation.

FOUR TIPS FOR BEING A GOOD FRIEND IN CRISIS

There are many resources for you, and at the same time we get to reach back and provide the same tender care and attention we need for those in our lives who need it most. Here are some good tips for helping a friend in crisis.

1. Be Present

Sometimes people don't need advice; they need presence. Offer to just hang out and do something fun with your friend. If they bring up the crisis or hard situation, let them guide it, but you just be present and bring peace to their heart.

2. Be Practical

Think of some ways you can practically help your friend. Grab lunch or dinner for them. Drop off groceries. Pay for their coffee or to get their nails done. Sometimes people in crisis don't really know what they need at the moment or how to answer, "What can I do to help?" Jump right in with a noninvasive way to provide comfort.

3. Be Curious

When your friend is ready to talk about the crisis, focus on being curious and asking open-ended questions. Avoiding yes-or-no questions helps to open up the conversation and create a safe space for them to share their feelings and feel seen and known. And instead of sharing a similar experience or feeling that you have had in the past, share how their feelings have made you feel. Example: "When you said that you were feeling sad that that person hurt you and left you, I felt so betrayed for you. I'm sorry you had to experience that."[1]

4. Be Prayerful

Prayer still works. And one of the greatest things you can do to stand alongside your friend in crisis is to remember where your strength comes from as you stand in the trenches with them. Our power comes from God; our ability to love comes from God because He is love. So be there in the natural and in the spiritual. And if they're comfortable with it, offer to pray while you're together.

NOTES

Introduction

1. Brené Brown, "The Power of Vulnerability," filmed June 2010 in Houston, TX, TED video, 20:03, https://www.ted.com/talks/brene_brown_the_power_of_vulnerability/transcript.
2. Curt Thompson, *Soul of Shame: Retelling the Stories We Believe About Ourselves* (Downers Grove, IL: IVP Books, 2015), 52.
3. Jennie Allen, *Find Your People: Building Deep Community in a Lonely World* (Colorado Springs, CO: WaterBrook, 2022), 165.

Chapter 5: Surrender

1. Jeanine Cox, *The Perfect Name: A Step-by-Step Guide to Naming Your Baby* (New York: Barnes and Noble Books, 2010), s.v. "Heather."
2. Tupac Aman Shakur, "The Rose That Grew from Concrete," in *The Rose That Grew from Concrete* (New York: Pocket Books, 1999), 3.

Chapter 6: Community

1. Based on *Oxford English Dictionary*, s.v. "shame," Lexico, accessed June 1, 2022, https://www.lexico.com/en/definition/shame.
2. Curt Thompson, *The Soul of Shame: Retelling the Stories We Believe about Ourselves* (Downers Grove, IL: IVP, 2015), 109.
3. *Oxford English Dictionary*, s.v. "community," Lexico, accessed June 1, 2022, https://www.lexico.com/definition/community.

4. Jenna Carver, *Hopeful Woman*, online course on Kajabi, https://brokencrayons.mykajabi.com/final-course-waiting-list.
5. Carver, *Hopeful Woman*.
6. Rick Thomas, "Do You Want My Attention or Do You Want My Care?," RickThomas.net, accessed May 17, 2022, https://rickthomas.net/do-you-want-my-attention-or-my-care-2/.

Chapter 7: Counseling

1. Eddie Kaufholz, "Going to Therapy Doesn't Mean You Have a Lack of Faith," *Relevant*, August 26, 2021, https://www.relevantmagazine.com/life5/does-going-therapy-mean-i-have-lack-faith/.
2. Curt Thompson, *Anatomy of the Soul: Surprising Connections Between Neuroscience and Spiritual Practices That Can Transform Your Life and Relationships* (Carol Stream, IL: Tyndale Momentum, 2010), 137.
3. Thompson, *Anatomy of the Soul*, 137.

Chapter 8: Gratitude

1. Jenna Carver, *Hopeful Woman*, online course on Kajabi, https://brokencrayons.ykajabi.com/final-course-waiting-list.
2. Oprah Winfrey, "What Oprah Knows for Sure About Gratitude," Oprah.com, accessed May 18, 2022, https://www.oprah.com/spirit/oprahs-gratitude-journal-oprah-on-gratitude.
3. Karrie Scott Garcia (@karriescottgarcia), Instagram Live streaming video, May 24, 2021, https://www.instagram.com/karriescottgarcia/.
4. Robert Holden, cited in Madhuleena Roy Chowdhury, "Giving Thanks: How Gratitude Affects the Brain," Aspen Brain Institute, accessed May 18, 2022, https://aspenbraininstitute.org/blog-posts/gratitudeandthebrain.
5. Madhuleena Roy Chowdhury, "The Neuroscience of Gratitude and How It Affects Anxiety and Grief," PositivePsychology.com, April 9, 2019, https://positivepsychology.com/neuroscience-of-gratitude/.
6. Jeff Henderson, "How to Get Better—Better, Part 1," published by North Point Community Church, January 8, 2019, YouTube video, 40:59, https://www.youtube.com/watch?v=lrFxvZGBpDs.

7. "Martin Seligman and Positive Psychology," Pursuit of Happiness, accessed May 18, 2022, https://www.pursuit-of-happiness.org /history-of-happiness/martin-seligman-psychology/.

Chapter 10: A Holy Tingle

1. Sandra Stanley, *Comparison Trap: A 28-Day Devotional for Women* (Alpharetta, GA: North Point Resources, 2015), quoted in "Comparison Trap," Bible.com, accessed June 1, 2022, https://www .bible.com/reading-plans/2169-comparison-trap/day/1.

Chapter 11: Hopeful Woman

1. "Harriet Tubman and the Underground Railroad," National Park Service, last updated March 11, 2017, https://www.nps.gov/articles /harriet-tubman-and-the-underground-railroad.htm; Harriet Tubman Underground Railroad, National Historical Park, Maryland, National Park Service, last updated April 18, 2022, nps.gov/natu /index.htm.
2. Brené Brown, "Grief and Finding Meaning with David Kessler," March 31, 2020, in *Unlocking Us*, podcast, MP3 audio, 46:04, https:// brenebrown.com/podcast/david-kessler-and-brene-on-grief-and -finding-meaning/.

Resources

1. This is a practice I learned in my confessional community with Curt Thompson and six other women.

ABOUT THE AUTHOR

Toni Collier is the founder of Broken Crayons Still Color, an international women's ministry that helps women process their brokenness and reclaim hope. She is a speaker, host of the *Still Coloring* podcast, and author of *Brave Enough to Be Broken* and a children's book *Broken Crayons Still Color*. It's her passion to show people that they can be both broken and beautiful as they work out their healing at the feet of Jesus. Toni and her husband, Sam, live in Atlanta with their daughter, Dylan, and son, Sam Jr.

OUR WEAKNESS CAN BE EXCHANGED
for HIS POWER.

OUR BROKENNESS
for HIS STRENGTH.

OUR CHILDHOOD WOUNDS
CAN BE TRANSFORMED INTO
ADULT SCARS THAT ARE

HEALED
AND
SEALED

WHEN OUR PAIN IS BROUGHT
INTO THE LIGHT, HOPE AND
HEALING CAN BE FOUND.

JESUS IS
CHOOSING
YOU RIGHT NOW.

IF WE'RE GOING TO
HEAL FROM IT,
WE'VE GOT TO NAME IT.

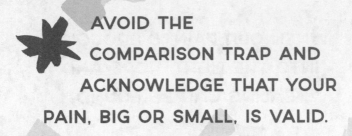 AVOID THE
COMPARISON TRAP AND
ACKNOWLEDGE THAT YOUR
PAIN, BIG OR SMALL, IS VALID.

THE ENEMY OF OUR
SOULS DOESN'T WANT
US TO BELIEVE THAT
GOD IS WITH US.

WHEN WE NAME OUR BROKENNESS
AND BOAST FREELY
ABOUT IT, WE FIND
FREEDOM IN CHRIST.

THERE'S NO BROKENNESS
GOD CAN'T REDEEM, *and*
THERE'S NO DARKNESS
THAT'S STRONGER THAN
THE LIGHT OF JESUS.

I'VE NEVER SEEN A HEALING JOURNEY
THAT HAS UNFOLDED
IN A LINEAR WAY

I HAD TO BELIEVE IN
A HEALER BEFORE I
COULD BE HEALED.

THE ENEMY'S  LIES

SOUND A LOT LIKE

GOD'S
TRUTH

HIDING IS THE
KRYPTONITE TO
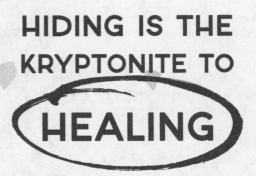
HEALING

SHAME SAYS YOU
DON'T DESERVE
HEALING AND
WHOLENESS.

THE ENEMY WILL TEMPT
YOU TO BELIEVE THAT GOD
WON'T TALK TO YOU *or*
THAT HE DOESN'T WANT TO.

COMMUNITY IS WHERE YOU
CAN FIND A REFLECTION OF
GOD'S GOOD INTENTIONS:
PEOPLE WHO KNOW &
LOVE YOU DEEPLY,
GOOD & BAD,
and AFFIRM YOUR BELONGING.

PEOPLE WON'T ALWAYS LOVE YOU WELL, BUT GOD ALWAYS WILL. XOXO

WE MUST TAKE OUR MENTAL AND EMOTIONAL HEALTH SERIOUSLY.

GOD IS ON YOUR SIDE IN THIS HEALING JOURNEY.

THE GOAL OF HEALING IS
FOR YOU TO BECOME
STRONGER IN YOUR MIND,
STRONGER IN YOUR HEART, ~~AND~~
STRONGER IN YOUR SPIRIT.

AND IF YOU ARE
GOING TO FIGHT
THE ENEMY, IT
WON'T REQUIRE
INTELLECT; IT
WILL DEMAND
YOUR KNEELING.

THE STRENGTH BENEATH THE LIES OF
THE ENEMY IS THAT HE BULLIES US
INTO BELIEVING WE ARE THE ONLY
ONES WHO HAVE FELT BROKEN.

TO COMBAT THE LIES OF THE
ENEMY, YOU'VE GOT TO BE
CLOSELY TETHERED TO GOD.

GRATITUDE
IS ONE OF THE
TOOLS YOU CAN
USE TO CLAW
YOUR WAY OUT
OF A VALLEY.

IT IS

VERY IMPORTANT

THAT YOU
HEAL BEFORE
YOU HELP.

WITH THE

POWER *of* JESUS

YOU ARE STRONGER THAN
YOUR BROKENNESS.